Dare to Dream

Inspirational insights for achieving
a successful and fulfilling life

CURT MARSH

True Colors, Inc. Publishing
Riverside, California

12395 Doherty Street
Riverside, California 92503

Library of Congress Card Number: 00-105578
ISBN 1-893320-21-9

Editor: Mike Berry
Book design: Michael Church
Printed and bound by Central Plains Book Manufacturers

Printed in the United States of America

CONTENTS

FOREWORD

We at True Colors are excited about this book and the potential it holds for every person who reads it, especially today's youth. Not only is Curt's triumphant story captivating and motivating, but it captures the very essence of the True Colors philosophy—to better understand and appreciate ourselves and the differences in those around us.

You are sure to be inspired as Curt leads you through his personal journey of victories and obstacles. And his insight and outlook on life will help you set goals for achieving a successful and fulfilling life. Lastly, I promise you this: You will be challenged!

So sit back, relax, and do yourself a favor. *Dare to Dream*!

—Don Lowry
True Colors Founder

INTRODUCTION

Curt Marsh is a 1977 graduate of Snohomish High School, in Washington state where he excelled as an athlete, especially in football. From Snohomish he moved on to the University of Washington where he played in three Bowl Games and two college all-star games for the Husky football team. After his senior season, Curt was selected as a college All-American, was named Lineman of the Year for the U of W, and was recognized as one of the best 100 football players in the school's history.

In 1981, Curt was the first-round draft pick of the Oakland Raiders. As a rookie, he became a starting offensive guard and was voted to the NFL All-Rookie Team. Throughout his career Curt was rated as one of the top players in the league at his position. The high point in his outstanding 7-year NFL career was his membership on the 1983 Raiders Super Bowl Championship Team.

Curt's NFL career was cut short in 1987 due to a severe ankle injury, which eventually led to the amputation of his right foot and ankle in 1994. After being fitted with an artificial leg, Curt was determined to not act "disabled" and started training to compete in events organized for wheelchair and amputee athletes. He set his sights on becoming a champion in the sport of weightlifting. He accomplished his goal, after a year of intense work, when he competed in the 1995 Wheelchair and Amputee National Championships and won the Gold Medal in power lifting. Curt's inspiring story has been featured on ESPN, CNN, and ABC's Nightline, and has been chronicled in many national publications, including a feature story in *Sports Illustrated*.

After retiring from the NFL in 1987, Curt volunteered as a public speaker to schools on behalf of the Traffic and Safety Commissions for Washington, Oregon, Idaho and Alaska. In 1990, he was hired as the youth programs coordinator for the City of Everett in Washington state. Yet Curt still found time to be a speaker and the state spokesperson for the Washington Interscholastic Activities Association's "High Five" drug and alcohol prevention program.

Curt continued to work for the City of Everett for nine years and ended his career there as the superintendent of recreation. As superintendent, Curt and his team won many prestigious local and national honors for outstanding service to youth. These successes led to Curt being invited to speak at State and National Parks and Recreation conferences to share his philosophy and tactics.

Curt began his professional speaking career as a part-time venture in 1991. Since that time, he has spoken to over half a million young people and thousands of adults and business groups throughout the United States and Canada, earning a reputation as a highly skilled motivational communicator.

In 1999, Curt retired from the City of Everett to pursue his passion for public speaking full-time and to undertake the challenge of becoming a successful writer. He currently lives in Snohomish, Washington, with his best friend and wife, Pam, their two teenage sons Jake and CJ, and wonderful daughter Jillian.

1

ROCK BOTTOM

". . . I was left with only two options: Amputate or live in horrible physical pain the rest of my life."

The familiar chill in the air coupled with the strong antiseptic smells had me feeling as though I were dreaming the same nightmare I had too many times before. The eerie silence in that familiar darkened hallway was nudged aside when the anesthesiologist quietly asked if I was beginning to feel the initial dose of pre-op medicines he had just pushed through my IV. Instead of the relaxing effect the drugs were supposed to provide, I was reminded of the reality of what I had chosen to put myself through this early September morning of the 35th year of my life. The reality was tempered with hope each of the prior twelve times the doctors and nurses had maneuvered me through this hallway. The hope was always that the impending surgery would restore a measure of mobility to my damaged ankle and finally provide some freedom from the excruciating pain. I did not hope for a complete healing, but just enough to allow me to walk, play, or maybe even run with my three active children.

On this, my thirteenth trip, it was different. Very definitely different, and I could feel it. As we neared the operating room doors I began to sense the building anxiety approaching a crescendo. It felt as though it had been growing in the pit of my stomach and slowly started to travel through my heart towards my throat. For one brief moment, I believed I would not be able to contain it. I imagined the anxiety rising to fill my cheeks and explode through my lips with a shout of *I can't do it. I just can't go through with it*! I pictured myself leaping from the gurney, breaking free of the doctors and nurses and limping as fast as I could down the hall, through the packed lobby and out to my car to escape the fate that awaited me. Somehow I found the courage to lay still and enter the operating room doors.

After nine grueling hours of surgery, a weary doctor emerged from the operating room. My wife, Pam, exhausted by the hours of struggling against the crushing weight of feeling powerless, could not help but notice the speckles and smears of blood on the surgeon's shoes as he approached. Tears welled up in her eyes with the recognition that the blood was most certainly mine and was conclusive evidence of what she had imagined was happening to her husband behind the operating room doors. The doctor assured my wife and the others still holding vigil that I was doing fine. He explained that the surgery was finished, and the staff was pleased with how well the operation had gone. It had been a complete success.

The fact that the operation had gone well and the doctor's reassurance that I was doing fine were of great comfort to Pam. However, she recognized the underlying significance of the surgeon's final words. She knew they also meant that I would never walk again without the aid of a prosthesis and had just begun my new life as an amputee.

In the recovery room I vaguely remember hearing someone softly calling my name. The sound was quiet at first and then became gradually louder, as if the person repeating my name were moving towards me. Finally, the loudest call was accompanied by a firm pat on my arm, and I came to consciousness. It took me a few moments to orient myself as the attending nurse described where I was and why I was there. As my thoughts came into focus, my heart felt as though it had sunk to my knees. I looked the nurse in the eye and asked, "Is it done?" She gave me a kind, reassuring look and nodded yes.

Even after acknowledging her answer, my first instinct was to try to wiggle my ankle and toes. To my amazement I felt them wiggle. I moved them once more, and again to my surprise I felt movement. My eyes widened and my heart began to race. I thought *My foot and ankle are still there. The doctors must have found another solution. They must have discovered a way of fixing my ankle without having to amputate.* I immediately sat up to visually confirm what my mind and heart told me but was shocked by what I saw. I caught just a glimpse before I fell back to my pillow, horrified. But the image of the deformed, bloody, bandaged stump where my foot and ankle should have been will stay etched in my heart and mind forever.

I do not cry easily. But at that moment, I began to cry. My crying turned to sobbing. I continued to sob as the nurse assured me that I would be fine. She explained that the physical feelings I described to her were phantom feelings or phantom pains, and they would probably persist for some time. I continued to cry. I cried that day until I could cry no more.

During the three weeks I spent in the hospital and the two months at home recovering, I had much time to think. It was hard to believe what had happened to me. I had for so long been known as "Curt Marsh the athlete" or "Curt Marsh the football player." A high school and college All-American, I was the first-round draft choice of the Oakland Raiders in 1981 and was the first rookie to start on the team's offensive line since Hall of Fame inductee Gene Upshaw, 16 years earlier. I was a starting offensive lineman playing guard for the Raiders for seven years and was rated amongst the top players in the league at my position. And I wear a Super Bowl ring from our 1983 NFL championship. Then came the career-ending ankle injury.

During my career with the Raiders I had my share of injuries. I had survived two lower back surgeries, two surgeries to repair broken bones in my left hand and right arm, and a few post-season orthroscopic surgeries to fix "minor" ligament, cartilage and bone damage in my knees and ankle.

In my last game on the active roster as a Raider, it should have been clear to me that my body was saying it was time for me to retire. We were playing against the Washington Redskins in Washington D.C., during the 1986 season. I had been suffering through terrible lower back spasms for weeks and they were hitting me hard during the entire first quarter and the beginning of the second, when I noticed a burning sensation on the bottom of both feet. It felt as though I was running on hot coals. I found out at half time that the new shoes I was wearing for that game had caused huge blisters that had formed over the balls of my feet and then ripped off, leaving the bare flesh underneath to grind into my socks with each agonizing step.

As an offensive lineman, my job was to use my hands, arms, legs, feet and any other part of my body to slow the 300-pound-plus defensive linemen from hitting and tackling my quarterback and running backs. As if the back pain and blisters were not enough, during a pass play late in the second quarter, I was blocking my opponent and felt my ankle twist and buckle under me. As I fell backwards, the teammate to my left pushed his defensive lineman in my direction and ran into me. As both of these huge, 300-pound men fell onto me they collapsed the outside of my left knee, twisting it inward as we all went down in a heap. I felt a tremendous amount of pain shoot through my left knee and a lesser amount pounding in my right ankle. I tried to stand up after the play, but my knee was too painful and would not support my weight. I knelt back down and waited for the trainers to come out on the field to help me.

When the trainers got me to the bench on our sideline, the team doctors started to test my knee for injury. The doctors began doing a range of motion test to see if there were any tears in the ligaments or cartilage that connect the bones and muscles of the leg and hold the knee in place. To do this, they straighten your knee and hold your foot straight out in front of you as you sit on the bench. They then start to move your ankle and shin from side to side as far as they can, using your knee as the fulcrum. This is done to test the sides of your knee. If there is too much movement, it is a sure sign that you have done some major damage to the soft tissue of your knee joint. Major injury in this area would require surgery and at least six months of rehabilitation. As they moved my left foot outward I realized that there was more movement in my knee joint than normal. The look on my teammate, Jamie Kimmel's, face as he watched the leg fan out to the side in an unnatural way confirmed that he thought something was wrong. I was told that there was obviously some ligament damage but we could not know how much without further tests.

In the meantime, the doctors treated the injury like they treated most of the injuries I had while playing for the Raiders. It actually seemed humorous at times because it reminded me of how I used to treat my very sensitive, older car when I was in college. If my car was not working properly, I would look into the problem one step at a time, hoping against all hope that it was nothing major. Even though it may have been inevitable, I did not want to know that I could not use my car or might have to spend a large amount of money and time to fix it. So I would start on the surface and only investigate and fix what I thought would be the simplest and least expensive solution and hope it worked. I would only delve further if the temporary solutions proved ineffective once the car was tested on the road.

In some ways, I had become that old car. The main job for the team doctors in the NFL is somewhat different than your neighborhood family physician. They are charged with keeping players healthy enough to play, not necessarily healthy in the way a normal person may understand the word. The owners hire and pay the doctors and expect their money's worth. Owners don't like to see high-priced players sitting on the sideline injured and unable to play.

The doctors taped me up and had me run up and down the sideline, hoping that the tape job would be a good enough fix to get me out on the field again. If that was successful, they would do further investigation later if they felt it was necessary. With this type of treatment, the body can only last for so long. But that is just the way it was. We all knew it. We all understood it. And, we all expected it. So, with their masterful tape job and my high tolerance for pain, I went back on the field and finished out the end of the second quarter.

At half time the trainers re-taped my knee and the doctors gave me a shot of Novocain to deaden the pain in my lower back. They then used a large syringe to draw the bloody fluid from my now very swollen right ankle and emptied that into a Dixie cup. Once the excess fluid was removed, they filled the syringe with Novocain and shot the ankle to deaden the pain before re-taping it. The next task was to cut the useless, ripped up skin from my feet and apply a felt-like product called Tuffskin over the exposed sores covering the balls of my feet. Some petroleum jelly was put in my socks to ease the friction before I put my shoes back on. Finally, I was ready to go out for the second half.

Throughout the third and fourth quarters, I was in excruciating pain. The game was very close and we needed a win badly to stay in the playoff race. Near the end of the fourth quarter we were down by two points with just over a minute to play. The offense had gotten the ball back on our own 30-yard line. All we needed to do was move the ball forty yards to the Redskins' 30-yard line to be close enough to kick a field goal and win the game. We did not have any time outs left and needed to run plays without a huddle. The quarterback, Marc Wilson, would yell out the play on the line of scrimmage, the ball was hiked and the play was run. After the play was over we would all hustle to the new line of scrimmage and listen for the next play. Repeating this over and over would save precious seconds and allow us time to run several plays to move the ball close enough for the winning field goal.

After the first three plays, we had one first down and were slowly moving the ball toward Washington's 30-yard line. During the next play I heard a loud snap and felt an intense pain in my right ring finger. After the play I looked at my hand and could not believe what I was seeing. My right ring finger had been broken, with the top half pointing in a completely different direction than the other fingers on my hand. I briefly thought about running off the field to have it looked at when a voice in my head said *What? After all the things you are playing through now—your back, knee, ankle and feet—are you really thinking of leaving the game for a little broken finger?* It seemed to me that with only seconds left in the game, and all the painful injuries I was already playing with, it would almost be embarrassing to run off the field simply because of a little broken bone in my hand. Lending support to the stereotype of the "dumb jock," I pulled on my injured finger, forcing the bone back into place and continued to play the remaining four plays of the game.

We came up short, not getting into field goal range, and ended up losing the game. There didn't seem to be enough ice in the locker room after the game to cover all the aches and pains I had. What a miserable five-hour plane ride back to the west coast that was. Looking back, I would have been smart to end my career right then and there.

After returning to Los Angeles, I went for some tests and found that I had indeed partially torn the medial collateral ligament in my knee. I was out for the season. The injury did not require surgery and we worked extremely hard through the rest of the season and the upcoming off-season to rehabilitate the knee. As the knee improved, the ankle became more and more of a focus. It was still swelling up after workouts and was extremely sore at times. The x-rays that the team took did not show any obvious breaks that the doctors could see. Their diagnosis was a simple ligament strain. And, as I described earlier, the doctors were not likely to look any further than they had to, as long as they could tape it up and I was able to work out on the ankle with a bearable amount of pain.

As the 1987 training camp approached, my ankle was still bothering me. Other than the ankle, I felt I was in good shape and was looking forward to playing again. But, as the first few days of training camp went by my ankle swelled up larger than it ever had before. I was once again having the ankle drained and then shot with Novocain just to be able to practice. After two days of this, I finally challenged the team doctors to look further into my ankle injury. I was convinced there was something terribly wrong and they weren't finding it. I was told there was no need to look further and that my injury was simply some ligament damage. They said that if I continued to play it would gradually get better. The next morning, I awoke to find my ankle so swollen and sore that I could barely walk. It was then that I demanded that the team let me leave training camp to go into Los Angeles and get some second opinions from doctors not associated with the Raiders football team.

The next day, I took the x-rays the Raiders had produced and went to see three different, well-known physicians in the Los Angeles area. All three said I should have a better set of x-rays done to diagnose the problem accurately. I chose one of the doctors to do the tests and the new films were done. The more intrusive type of x-rays showed that there was something very wrong. The talus bone in my right ankle was broken clear through and had been grinding on the joint surfaces around it. No one could know, for sure, how long it had been broken. However, the doctor said that wear on the joint surfaces surrounding the talus suggested that it had been broken for some time. It could have possibly started as a stress fracture as far back as the 1986 Redskins game when the ankle twisted and buckled. I was informed that surgery would be required to fix the bone. My season was over before it even started. I decided to allow the doctor who made the correct diagnosis to do the surgery.

The first surgery was a simple fix. They just needed to put a couple of screws through the bone so that it would grow back together and heal. I had a very severe reaction to the anesthesia. I woke from the surgery with a terrible headache and threw up immediately. These symptoms continued for an additional three days. I have never felt so terrible, for so long, in all my life. At one moment during the post surgery ordeal I told my wife I never wanted to go through this again and if I ever mentioned playing football when this was over, she was to shoot me. Soon after my recovery, I confirmed that I was finished with professional football and the injuries. It was time to retire while I thought I was ahead. At that time, I believed the choice was mine. I had no idea that I could not have returned to football again even if I had wanted to. I did not know that after retirement there would be much more pain and suffering. And, I certainly had no clue that this ankle injury would so drastically change my life forever.

The initial surgery to repair the bone proved to be a success. However, complications in removing the screws months later led to an infection and a three-week stay in the hospital on IV antibiotics.

The ankle required another surgery about a year later to remove new bone spurs and chips which continued to form due to the prior injuries. Again, an infection resulted following this surgery. I spent an additional two weeks in the hospital and several weeks at home on IV therapy. Over the years there were more surgeries attempting to fix the ankle, all of which proved to be failures. Six years and twelve surgeries later, I faced an enormous challenge. The bone was so damaged by the initial injury and the subsequent infections that I was left with only two options: amputate or live in horrible physical pain the rest of my life.

I don't mean to make it sound as though we just went from surgery to surgery, sitting and waiting for the next one. We were an active, growing family during those six years. After leaving football in 1987, I started a small vending business. Three years later I sold a bigger, successful vending business. In 1990, I accepted an offer to work for the City of Everett in Washington state as a youth programs coordinator under their human services department. Pam went to work for the city as well, and later used her highly praised customer service skills to help the family financially by working for a home medical supply company. With both of us working, things were hectic at home, but we managed to continue raising our family and excelling at our jobs. As I grew more adept at working with high-risk kids and within the governmental process, I was promoted to the youth coordinator position at the Everett Parks Department. I continued to receive praise from my superiors, while earning a reputation as a good leader who could motivate others to accomplish personal and organizational goals. Soon I was promoted to superintendent of recreation with responsibilities for all of the recreation functions of the Everett Parks Department.

In addition to my job, I was speaking at as many schools and youth group functions as I could. I was blessed with both a desire and gift to be able to effectively communicate with youth of all ages and encourage them to make good choices in their lives. All this time, our own children were struggling, succeeding, and growing.

With a busy life, it was unusual to have the three weeks lying in the hospital room with ample time to just think. During that time I contemplated some very serious questions. Who am I now? What am I going to do with my life now? Where do I start from here? What will it take for me to successfully overcome this? These are not unusual questions. As a matter of fact, we often ask ourselves these kinds of questions when we hit the potholes in life's journey. But this time it seemed more real and more intense than ever before. The more I struggled to create new answers to these very old questions, the harder it was to see answers at all.

Then, one night while praying, I began to consider the previous challenges I had experienced and how I had overcome them. I looked back on those areas of my life where I had experienced a measure of pain and failure followed by success. I searched to identify the principles that guided me to those successes. With those recollections my confidence grew. I realized that the answers to my questions did not have to be so complicated. I had done this before. And with that, I first began to believe I would be able to do it again. Lying there, looking up at the ceiling in the darkness of my hospital room, I began to challenge myself to put into motion those same guiding principles I had used in the past.

In addition, I had learned new lessons about life that were truly empowering. The entire amputation experience opened my eyes to insights I might not have ever learned otherwise. These new pearls of wisdom would be added to past principles to be the foundation that would support my achieving the rich, fulfilling, successful life that was still awaiting me.

This book defines those principles I have used in the past and the lessons I have more recently learned to enable me to strive for such a life. I have not written an autobiography. I have simply attempted to share with you the important set of truths that I believe are essential for any one of us to build a life that we can ultimately be proud of living.

The choice of how you use this information is obviously yours. Many things happen to us in this life that we cannot control. However, we do have control of our thoughts, beliefs and behaviors. It is my hope that by reading the following chapters, you will discover some reasons to get excited about achieving not only what life has to offer you, but also what you have to offer in return. I am hopeful that these words will not only encourage you to think, but also to believe and behave in ways that will help you establish and accomplish your dreams regardless of your circumstances.

2

LESSONS LEARNED THE HARD WAY

"I believe that we innately possess the capacity to deal with whatever happens to us."

When people discover that my career in professional football caused the injury which led to my amputation, I am often asked *Would you do it again*? *Would you play Pro Football*? My answer is a most positive and definite *Yes*! It was my dream, what I had worked so hard for. It was my opportunity to be the best in the world at something. My son asked me once how many people had a Super Bowl championship ring. I had never thought about it, so I sat down and figured that if there were thirty Super Bowls and fifty guys on a team, the answer would be somewhere around 1,500 guys. I was certainly proud of the ring before, but it wasn't until that moment that I realized just how fortunate I was to own one. If I were to do it over, knowing then what I know now, I might change a doctor or two or not play with some injuries. But the answer would still be *Yes*!

A second question often follows the first and that is *But, wouldn't you want to have your leg back*? My sarcastic response is usually *Heck no. I love getting up in the middle of the night to go to the bathroom, forgetting I don't have a leg and tipping over. That's great fun. I love it when I take off my prosthesis, fall asleep, and wake up to find my kids have hidden it. It's a "barrel of monkeys" crawling around the house looking for the rest of your body*. Of course the real answer is that I would love to have my leg back. However, I like who I am now more than I ever have in my life. Much of the increased self-respect has come from what I learned through the amputation process, before and after. So, if getting my leg back would mean losing the lessons I have learned to help me get where I am mentally and spiritually today, the answer to the second question would be a resounding *No*! It would not be worth having my leg back to give up what I've gained.

I am sure that others who have been through trying times have learned similar lessons. I am hopeful that by sharing the ones I have learned, some may benefit without having to learn them the hard way. I embrace these truths as if they were precious pearls that I have discovered. Although the experiences, which taught them to me, were disheartening at the time, I cherish the encouragement they have already given me.

I have always lived my life believing I was going to be someone special. I had two parents who loved me. We were not rich, but we did have all we needed. I was generally successful in those areas where I applied myself. No one in my immediate family went through any unusual illness or suffering. I really had not had to face something in my life that I could not overcome with a positive attitude or determination. But that changed when I learned I had to have my leg cut off. No matter how positive my attitude or how determined I was, I could not save my leg.

I had come to a point in my life when I finally had to admit that there were some things out of my control and that there are times when this life just really "sucks." One of the greatest lessons I have learned through this experience is that there is always good news and bad news. The bad news is that we are all going to face those times in our lives when things happen that just aren't fair. Disease, abuse, neglect, losing loved ones, and even smaller things like being forced to have sections of your body removed because of the mistakes of others are never happy times. These experiences shouldn't happen to anyone. Yet no matter who you are or what you do during your lifetime, you will experience times that bring this kind of pain. Sometimes these cruel and agonizing experiences can even bring you to the point of asking yourself *Is this life even worth the pain*?

Now for the good news. The good news is simple. Life is not, was not, and never will be about what happens to you. Life—the very essence of life itself—is, was, and always will be about how you choose to respond to what happens to you.

The second lesson I learned gave me the courage to act on the first one. I was lying in my bed one morning when I noticed an annoying sound coming from the upper left-hand corner of my room. I looked up and discovered it was coming from the two foil balloons that someone had brought me the day before. Both of the balloons were twisted together and located right by the air conditioner. With the airflow they would bounce back and forth on the ceiling, making this incredibly nerve-racking sound. I called the nurse and she moved them away from the air conditioner. I shut my eyes and the next thing I knew, the balloons adorned with *I Love You* and *Get Well Soon* were back at the air conditioner and driving me nuts again. I called the nurse and asked her to throw them away. She refused as they were a gift from a loved one, and she told me I would have to do it. Yeah right. What was I going to do? Hop over? Remember this was a couple of days after my surgery, and I was mad at the Raiders, God, and anyone or anything else that I encountered. I was swimming in a pool of self-pity, feeling so terribly sorry for myself that I was in danger of drowning.

My wife finally walked into the room, and I immediately demanded that she throw those annoying balloons in the garbage. My wife is a strong, confidant woman who quickly responded by saying, "Are you talking to me? Did you really think you were talking to me? No, I didn't think so." I then explained the situation calmly, and she came up with the idea of us taking them up to the children's ward to give them to one of the kids who might appreciate them a little more than I did. I was not too keen on getting my butt in the wheelchair and going up two floors to deliver the balloons. I was still hurting pretty badly both inside and out. But my wife got the wheelchair, told me to squeeze my large behind into it, and off we went.

When the elevator doors opened to Harborview Medical Center of Seattle's children's floor I was surprised to hear laughing. It sounded like only one child's laughter, but it was so boisterous that it filled the hall. It wasn't a giggle or even a belly laugh. It was like one of those laughs that happen only when you are not supposed to laugh—like when you are in class at school. You struggle, doing everything in your power to hold it in. The worst is when the person next to you is in on it, and you can't hear or even see him without losing it. Then you glance his way and catch a glimpse of his shoulders bobbing up and down and you explode. The laughter comes out of your face through every hole available and it's huge and loud. It was that kind of laugh.

A little surprised but not moved by the laughter, I pushed toward the nurse's station where a nurse was on the phone. I pointed up and kind of mouthed the question, "Is there anyone here who would like these balloons?" She nodded and pointed over her shoulder. I had to lift myself up on my chair a little to see over the counter and was amazed by what I saw.

There sat a little boy, maybe nine years old. I noticed he had some kind of nylon material on his head. Then I noticed he had no hair. Looking at his eyes, I could see that one of his eyelids was missing and the other one only half there. I'd say his nose was deformed except there really was no nose at all. There were just two holes where his nose was supposed to be. He was on the phone so I looked at his mouth and noticed that he had no lips. His teeth and gums were fully exposed and there was a lot of scaring everywhere. This little boy had obviously survived a terrible fire. Lastly, I noticed that he was not holding the phone with his hand, as you or I normally would, but instead between two stumps that started about two inches below his elbows. He had found a way to use them to squeeze the phone and push it up to what was left of his ear. Then it happened. That same laughter again, only now I could see where it was coming from. It was coming from him. At that moment every fiber of my body remembered something I had been told when I was young. Someone had told me not to complain about my circumstances because I would not have to look very far to find someone a little worse off than myself. I saw the courage and resiliency of that little boy, who had found something to be joyous about even in his frail, deformed situation. At that moment I thought to myself *Curt, there is nothing wrong with you.*

Bad things happen to good people. But I believe that we innately possess the capacity to deal with whatever happens to us. We just have to look within ourselves and find the courage like that little boy did.

I have never met that young man; I was so moved that I dropped off the balloons and had to leave. It is probably a good thing I haven't seen him since, because I would probably hug the poor kid so hard I would kill him. However, I am eternally grateful for his lesson and inspiration.

My wife taught the third lesson to me through her words and actions. I learned that it would not matter if I had gotten both legs cut off, or both arms, or my head (Well . . . no, I think I would still need the head.) Losing the rest of these body parts would not be that big of a deal, other than the physical inconvenience, because they have nothing to do with *who* I am.

Nearly twenty years ago, Pam married a 21-year-old, first-round draft pick of the Oakland Raiders, who was 6 feet, 5 inches tall and weighed 280 pounds with very little body fat. Eighteen years later, she goes to bed every night with an overweight 40-year-old man with half a leg which I shake at her every night saying, "Say goodnight to Stumpy." And still, this woman tells me that she loves me more now than she ever has. She explained that she loves *me*, not my body, but who I am inside. Boy, did that get me thinking. I thought *Wow, that must be how God sees us*. Then I asked myself, "What if I could see everyone else that way?" I started to look at people differently, beginning with my own family. When we would pass in the house, I would look into their eyes and try to ignore any of their bodily features until I could see them as they really were. I tried to look into the soul inside, the soul that will live somewhere forever. Soon, I began doing this with acquaintances and then strangers. As I looked past the shell to their innermost being, I began to be able to connect and feel a kinship with others, and show genuine care and concern for everyone I saw.

Recently, I was reminded of this lesson through the words of a song written and sung by a 7-year-old girl on an early morning television show. The show was about children who had gone through incredible challenges in their young lives and the impact these obstacles have had on them. This particular young lady had sparkling, vibrant, beautiful eyes in which you could see the dancing thoughts and emotions of any other young, happy child. Below her eyes and nose her face was not as pretty. This little girl had also suffered the trauma of surviving horrible burns, which had scarred her entire body three years prior to the show. Although very healthy now, she suffered terrible scars on her lower cheeks, lips and chin which formed her face into an unusual shape. As much as I was drawn by her cute, smiling answers to the interviewer's questions and those big bright eyes, I found it difficult to look past the grotesque markings on her face and arms. The scarring gave this little girl a look that some might describe as monstrous.

The interviewer finally asked a question that did not get the usual cute response. He paused and took a deep breath as if he didn't want to ask the next question but knew he must. He asked if she had any friends. A cloud seemed to come over the little girl's face as she tried to maintain her composure. Her eyes began to fill with tears and her lower lip poked out just a little and started to tremble. She was trying desperately not to cry as she looked down and shook her head no. The child's mother sitting next to her started to cry. You could see the compassion on the interviewer's face and hear it in his voice as he asked the next question. Leaning towards her and putting his hand on hers, he asked her why she didn't have friends. Her heartbreaking response came through the tears that were now freely flowing from her eyes, down her cheeks and over her lips. She said in a quiet, broken voice, "I don't know." I was questioning why the host would put her through this. I began to understand when he asked her if she had written a song and would like to sing it. The little girl wiped her eyes, shook her head yes, and reached into her pocket. She bravely stood up and unrolled a piece of paper with the wide-ruled lines used by young children just learning to write. She wiped her eyes, took a deep breath, and began to read from it as she sang. I could vaguely see the letters through the paper she was holding. The penmanship looked as if the words were written by her own hand. She steadied herself and in an absolutely beautiful little voice sang these words: "Please, don't make fun of me. Please don't call me names. Don't find your pleasure in my pain. Because when God looks at us, we all look the same."

I could only imagine the terrible pain that the stares, whispers and teasing of others had caused this little girl. Her outer shell had been damaged and was not as lovely as it once was. The little girl inside had not changed one bit. That little girl just wanted to be respected and loved. It was horrible to be reminded that we as human beings have the capacity to be so cruel.

Recently, I was at a junior high to do an assembly in the school gymnasium. The adult leader was out front trying to work the kids into an enthusiastic frenzy. He was leading cheers with the help of about twenty 8th grade leaders who were standing in front with him. The rest of the students were purposely smashed together, sitting on bleachers that were filled to capacity. As a matter of fact, there were several kids on the floor in front of the lowest bench. I had noticed a particular girl, sitting on the floor, who had been one of the last kids in the gym. She was very overweight and obviously not dressed in the stylish type of clothes most of the girls were wearing. She chose the floor rather than squeezing into one of the tiny slivers of room in the bleachers. She had looked for a seat, but every time she came to an empty space a kid would either move over or tell her it was saved. As the girl walked away, I could see the other children laughing and pointing at her.

After the cheers, the adult sent the leaders diving into the crowd and told everyone to make room for them to sit, as he wanted everyone in the stands for my presentation. He saw the few kids that were on the floor and told them that they had to squeeze up into the bleachers. The smaller children were able to find some spots as kids moved to make more room. But everywhere this obese young lady looked, kids glared back at her as if to say *There is no way you are going to sit by me*. My heart broke as the girl tried to make the best of it and crouched down at the end of the bottom bleacher to look as if she had found a seat. She yearned desperately to be a part of a group that obviously did not want to include her because of the difference in her outer shell. As the leader began my introduction I couldn't take it any longer. I left the gym in the middle of his first paragraph and found a comfortable chair. I brought it back, walked straight up to that sweet young girl, and told her that someone as special as her should not have to stand. I looked into her eyes and told her how pretty they were. Even though this gesture of kindness had made her smile, I could still see the hurt and pain that years of teasing, taunting, and laughter had scarred her with. All she wanted was for someone to treat her as though she meant something. Yet because she was different or not very attractive to the eye, others felt it was all right to hurt her, that somehow it was OK to throw her dignity to the ground and step on it. The human capacity to love is sometimes greatly diminished by our capacity to be cruel to others.

How many times do we avoid or discount someone simply based on an impression from seeing them only as their outer shell? I want you to try something. Start trying to see people for who they really are and not just the skin suit they wear. If you are able to look past the color of skin, the tattoos, the fat or skinny, the short or tall, and the piercing, and see the person inside, you will be touched. Look into their eyes to see the person they really are. It is like looking into a mirror as you begin to see yourself in that other person. We are not that much different. We all have the same desires to be free, to love and be loved, to be respected and encouraged and so many other similarities. I challenge you to see someone for who he or she really is beyond his or her outer appearance and not feel some twinge of care and concern for them. Since learning this lesson, I have committed myself to acting on it. My capacity to care for all of those I meet has increased dramatically. I am compelled to treat people differently when I am looking into their soul. What a tremendous gift it has been to see others who, regardless of their physical appearance, look just like me.

The fourth and final lesson was taught to me by all of those who called, wrote, and came by the hospital during my ordeal. The lesson was what goes around comes around. I had heard that saying many times before and had always interpreted it to mean that if you do something bad, it would come back to haunt you. In this context it means just the opposite.

During the time I was in the hospital, hundreds of people came to the room, sent letters and gifts, or called on the phone. Hundreds upon hundreds of people; I didn't know I knew so many people. Some I had known for years, others I had known very briefly, and some I had just met once. But every time it was the same message: *I just wanted to let you know I care about you, and you are in our thoughts and prayers*. I have often wondered, when attending funerals packed with well-wishers, *Did that man or woman have any idea while they were alive that this many people cared about them? If so, what a great feeling that would be*. I was given the opportunity to feel that kind of overwhelming love, and it was incredible.

There were two times I really let loose and cried while I was in that hospital. The first, which I described in the introduction, was right after the amputation. The second was when the nurses announced that they were about to do something they don't have to do very often. They were going to put a sign on my door not allowing visitors certain times of the day, even during visiting hours. They were also going to have to shut the phone off for those times because I was not getting enough rest to heal. I felt an overwhelming sense of humility and unworthiness. The tears came; I could not imagine that there were so many people who cared enough about me to take their own time and show it. I confessed to my wife that I didn't do anything that special for any of them that I could remember. She told me she thought the reason so many people responded when they heard what I was going through was not because of any huge thing I had done. Instead, she believed it was in response to one of the things that first drew her to me in high school. My wife went on to describe me as genuinely nice to people.

She explained how I seemed to care about them and their feelings from the first moment that I met them, and that they could tell. It was that simple.

If she's right, then it is true. What goes around does come around. And if that is true, the way we treat each individual every single day is how we will be treated when we need people most. How are you treating those around you today?

These lessons were learned through the pain and agony of questioning who I was and who I was going to be in the future. All at once, I was forced to face the most frightening and challenging changes I had ever experienced. As I look back now, I can appreciate and even embrace these changes because they have influenced my life for the better.

3

EMBRACING CHANGE

"How we perceive change has a great effect on how we respond when we encounter it."

The amputation experience and the adjustments to my life afterward have had an incredible effect on how I now perceive and respond to change. Change can be a powerful motivator. Many times in our lives we are challenged to rethink our dreams, goals, and actions in response to a string of events or even one single incident. Sometimes the need to change or readjust comes as a result of the consequences of choices we have made or as a response to something completely beyond our control.

Change constantly challenges us to adjust our life settings. It forces us to consider the redirecting of our own behavior. After my amputation and recovery story was recounted on television and in *Sports Illustrated*, I received a request from a psychologist who was authoring a book about people whom he felt had certain ingredients in their makeup that would define them as having a "survivor's personality." When I learned he wanted to do a story on me, I was flattered to be considered among that group of individuals. Then it occurred to me that I want to be remembered as more than just a "survivor." I aspire to be remembered as a "thriver."

My hope is that when I am laid to rest and people talk about the type of person I was, they would include something like, *No matter what happened to Curt or what changes occurred in his life, somehow he always seemed to come out on top.*

This more than hopeful attitude must be the reason my wife looks at me after I espouse some confident statement in the midst of a catastrophe and says, "There you go again. You are the King of wishful thinking!" I could think of worse things to be called.

Change is inevitable. Recent studies show that the average worker will go through at least five career changes during his/her working life. At the age of 40 I am embarking on my fifth career change by speaking full-time and authoring this book. One could say that I, like most, am no stranger to change. How I perceive change and respond to it, though, is different than before.

We all have perceptions of what the word "change" means, and we have emotions connected to those perceptions. While working for the City of Everett, I went through a very helpful supervisory training which emphasized the importance of this point. The instructor had us participate in an exercise aimed at teaching us something about how the average person perceives change. We were asked to pair up with someone we did not know very well. He then directed us to face each other and study our partner's appearance for an entire minute. We were told not to look away, even if it felt uncomfortable. This was not an easy thing to do. One minute seemed more like five. Finally, he directed us to face away from our partner and change three things about our appearance that would be noticeable. He continued to say that after a while he would ask us to face each other again and identify the three changes made by our partner to their own appearance.

Everyone turned around and immediately started taking off watches, hair clips, jackets, glasses, etc. When we were instructed to turn back around, my partner noticed that I had taken off my hat, watch and jacket. I noticed that she had removed her hair tie and glasses, and rolled up her sleeves. It seemed like a fairly simple exercise and I wasn't quite getting the point yet. The instructor then asked us to stare at one another for an additional minute and repeat the exercise. This time changing five more things about our appearance.

When it came time for us all to turn and inspect our partners, I found that my partner had only changed a couple of things. She said to me in a whisper, "I couldn't think of anything else I was willing to take off." While attempting my own transformation, I had discovered the same problem but looked over at the table and saw the banana I had brought to snack on. I decided I would have the banana sticking out of the top of my shirt; that would be a change. I also thought I might get a chuckle out of my partner. So I unbuttoned a couple of buttons and shoved the banana in stem first so it was protruding from my shirt and touching my chin.

The instructor complimented me on my ingenuity and then let us know that he was planning on having us do the exercise again. This time he wanted us to make ten changes to our appearance, none of which could include putting back on what we had already taken off. At this point I thought I might have an idea of his motive. I soon learned I wasn't the only person thinking along those lines when a woman near the front said, "That's impossible. There is no way I can make ten more changes without taking some clothes off, and I'm not going to do that." The instructor then stated that he would be able to do it without removing one stitch of clothing. He went on to say it would be no problem for him to make even twenty more changes. The woman challenged him to prove it. He agreed and started picking up different colored paper clips and fastening them to the pocket of his shirt. Each paper clip counted as one change.

The point was clear, and the instructor helped us to understand it even better with his explanation. When the average human being hears the word change, he tends to automatically think of it as taking away. Most don't see it in terms of adding. How we perceive change has a great effect on how we respond when we encounter it. If we perceive it negatively we respond defensively and are more resistant. When we perceive change in a positive way, we are much more likely to engage it with a positive attitude.

Looking back on my career changes, none was harder than the experience that occurred during the transition from professional football to owning a private business. After retiring from football and moving back to the Pacific Northwest, I was advised by some good friends of mine to invest in the vending business. I took their advice and became a vendor, buying machines and finding locations for them to sell candy, pop, and other snacks. I made money in this venture but learned a powerful lesson about the importance of choosing work that provides you with satisfaction other than just monetary gain. I learned the most fortunate professionals are those who are able to make a living doing something for which they feel passion. The snack vending business did nothing for my passions . . . except the one to eat. (It was not a good idea to store the inventory in my garage.) Though it was tough, I made several efforts to get excited about my business and even worked on developing catchy phrases for promotion. But I knew I was in trouble when the best I could come up with were slogans like *Don't take candy from strangers, buy it from me*!

The most visible influence the candy business had on me, as one might suspect, was the change that was happening to my body. Prior to my senior season at the University of Washington, after months of training, I ran the mile in 5 minutes and 32 seconds. Not bad for a man weighing 290 pounds. During my fourth year in pro football, at a weight of 280 pounds, I was measured as having less than 7 percent body fat. I placed fifth in the 1982 World's Strongest

Man Competition. I was first runner-up two years in a row at the NFL Arm Wrestling Championships in Las Vegas, and at one time in my career I could bench-press well over 500 pounds.

Today, still 6 feet, 5 inches tall but weighing a not-so-solid 350 pounds, I am suffering from what I call the "landslide theory." This is where the huge muscles that I had developed in my shoulders and chest to accomplish all of the athletic endeavors of my past are simply sliding down toward the mid-section of my body. I was not that concerned until a few months ago when I stepped out of the shower, bent over to dry my feet, and water poured out of my belly button. There was a lot of water in there, as if someone had thrown a bucket full into my bathroom.

At that point I did something that I had been avoiding for several years. I turned and looked at myself in the mirror naked, and it scared me! Not just the sight itself, but at that moment I experienced a full-blown "Fridge" flashback right there in my bathroom. I'm sure you've all heard of "Nam" flashbacks or "LSD" flashbacks. The dreaded Fridge flashback is a phenomenon experienced by offensive lineman of the 1980s who had the opportunity to play against a defensive tackle with the Chicago Bears by the name of William "The Refrigerator" Perry, a.k.a. "The Fridge."

It is difficult for the average person to really understand how large this human being actually was. For instance, I know for a fact that he was at least 6 feet, 4 inches. I don't know how tall he was, but that was his measurement from side to side. He was reported to weigh well over 400 pounds. I'll give you one comparison to help you understand this man's amazing proportions. The ring I wear from the 1983 Super Bowl is a size 14, a big ring because I am a very large man. The Fridge wears a Super Bowl ring from the 1985 championship game. His is a size 22! His fingers, like the rest of his body, are huge. They look like those giant beef sticks you buy from Hickory Farms at Christmas time.

People have often asked what it was like to block The Fridge. My answer always describes the experience as being very strange. You would run into him and then suddenly become surrounded by his mass, and everything would get dark. At that point you would usually begin to panic and start pushing and prodding everywhere, not in an effort to block him, as your coach was hopeful you might be trying to do, but simply struggling to find a way out. It really didn't smell very good in there. The scariest thing in this whole situation was that The Fridge was an incredibly gifted football player. Even with all his size, he could move quickly enough to make you look like a fool.

So there I was, standing in my bathroom and suddenly it occurred to me that I had heard William Perry was on a television show discussing his weight problem with a doctor who had diagnosed him as having an eating disorder. I started making the connection and got a little worried. The next day I set an appointment to see my doctor. He ran me through a complete regimen of tests. When I had finished the last one, my doctor invited me to sit with him so he could explain eating disorders and share the results of his findings. He began by explaining a disorder called Anorexia. This is when people constantly see themselves as fat no matter how skinny they are. They barely eat anything and are addicted to exercise. By this time my doctor saw the scrunched look on my face and said, "Don't worry, Curt. You don't have that one." He went on to describe Bulimia. A typical person with this disorder stuffs himself with unbelievable amounts of food, as much as 10 or 11 full meal deals at different drive-through restaurants, one after another. At the conclusion of this enormous feast he purges. This is a nice way of saying that after stuffing himself he makes himself throw it up.

At this point my doctor got more serious as he shared that he had diagnosed me with a dangerous eating disorder that should not be taken lightly. In this book you will read of my many triumphs, some of my proudest and strongest moments. Therefore, I feel it is only fair to share with you a few of my weaknesses as well. The clinical name for my particular type of eating disorder is "Bulimic Amnesia." It's where I stuff myself with unbelievable amounts of food and then just forget to throw it up. At least it's a diagnosed medical disorder now and I can get help. I've joined a twelve-step group. We stand around, talk, eat doughnuts, and then forget what to do next.

I soon began setting new fitness goals and taking steps toward accomplishing them. My first goal was to stand straight up and be able to look down and see my feet. But after a couple of weeks of looking down and realizing my feet were still nowhere in sight, I just decided to go out and buy bigger shoes. It became obvious I needed to find a better motivation to lose weight, and not just focus on giving up the food and snacks I loved.

The negative aspects of being overweight have been nagging at me to change, but it has been the focus on the positive outcomes that has allowed me the courage and motivation to make a commitment. I love and respect the person I have become, and I certainly love and respect my wife and children. The more I can do to spend as much time with them on this earth, the better. I want to enjoy the fruits of my hard-earned life lessons, so I must look at the changes I make to live a healthy lifestyle for what they will add to my life—not just focus on all the good food I am going to miss. Now in times of weakness, I concentrate on the positives I am going to gain through this change, rather than focusing on things I am forced to lose.

Embracing change in a positive way is not always this easy. When my ankle and foot were amputated, I felt as though something of great value had been ripped from me forever. I had not only lost the limb, but its function as well. Even more devastating than the physical loss was my belief that by losing my leg I had also somehow lost my ability to be an athlete and, even worse, a "normal" person. I saw myself as ugly and less than whole. At times I felt useless because of my inability to perform some of the simplest of daily tasks that I had always taken for granted.

The three months recovering at home were a monumental struggle for me. I was virtually immobile. The inability to put pressure on my stump or bear any weight on my right leg meant that I was confined to a wheelchair for weeks. As my wounds healed, I slowly graduated to being able to crawl and attempt to use a walker to get around by myself. Both of these methods were still extremely painful. I was forced to completely rely on my family members to bring me what I needed or to help me with even the smallest of chores. My wife had to help me dress myself daily. The most degrading and humiliating experiences were when my wife had to assist me in accomplishing the most personal of activities that we all prefer to do alone in the bathroom. The need to rely on other people for so many things was the most difficult change I had to deal with. I was deeply frustrated with the inability to retrieve things for myself or function independently. At times I would attempt to be self-sufficient because of my growing hatred of being dependent on others. I would usually end up in a painful, crumpled heap on the floor calling for someone to come and help me or clean up what I had dropped in my attempt to be self-reliant. I can remember losing it more than once and, with tears in my eyes as I lay on the floor, throwing my walker at the wall in frustration after another failed attempt to help myself. The realities of the constricting limitations I was being forced to accept caused me much more pain emotionally than even the worst of the physical pain.

The choice of how you spend the energy of your life is always yours. It is up to you and only you to choose to live life as a victor or a victim. Suppose the world's population could be divided in half, based on those who are constantly focusing on the problems and those who, while acknowledging the problems, constantly focus on the solutions. The individuals looking at the problems only behave as victims. These are people who ultimately will end up with little or no hope for the future based on the reality of their unfortunate circumstances. On the other side, there are those who use their energy and time focusing on finding solutions to these problems. This group of individuals will naturally behave as victors. They consciously choose to spend their life looking through their circumstances toward a dream of a better future. Their lives will be filled with hope and opportunity as they can see beyond the challenges.

After making the decision to become a problem solver and not just a problem identifier, it is extremely important that we don't simply look past the problem or ignore it in our attempts to overcome it. To really become the victor, we must work *through* the problem. This is a truth that I learned only recently while working to move past the pain of the physical and emotional changes I experienced before and after my amputation.

Isn't it interesting how some of the most valuable life lessons are best learned and retained through confronting, enduring, and surviving extremely painful experiences? As I think back, I realize that I have always found the courage to face the physical challenges in my life. At the same time I was being brave physically, I would do everything I could to avoid having to feel any of the emotional pain I encountered. I would try to ignore it, bury it, or sometimes just run from it. And I am not referring to the pain caused by my football injuries only, but to all the pain that I have felt in my life.

I can visualize myself growing from a young boy into a man, never wanting to feel the hurtful emotions that life sometimes dishes out. The act of embracing any grief or emotional agony was something I emphatically chose not to do. Instead, I would concentrate my energies on using my skills and abilities to rise above any self-doubt, criticisms or failures I encountered. I would simply try to look past the uncomfortable feelings and on to the next task. I would choose to ignore the problem rather than confront it and be subjected to feeling it. While having the desire and fortitude to rise above challenging situations is completely honorable, it is only part of the answer. By never allowing ourselves to experience the grief and sorrow that occur, we can never really overcome the hurt. We end up stuffing it somewhere in our hearts where it can and will come back to haunt us for years to come.

Thinking of this reminds me of some advice one of my college football coaches once gave me. Some teammates and I were visiting with this coach soon after he had gone through a divorce from his wife of ten years. One of the players asked if the long days and weekends away from home were the cause of the breakup. The coach shared that he really could not identify any one thing. He had concluded, after seeing a counselor, that during the marriage each had simply accumulated too much unresolved emotional baggage. It was as if he and his wife were wearing backpacks throughout their marriage. At the beginning of the relationship, both packs were empty. As the relationship progressed, normal marital problems began to occur. Instead of facing those situations head-on and choosing to endure the pain of really working together to resolve them, they would either ignore them as too trivial to fight about or run from having to deal with them at all. He said that those unresolved issues were thrown in their packs and therefore out of sight. As time went by, other painful incidents would occur but never be resolved, and the packs continued to get a little heavier each time.

Over the years, those backpacks became too heavy to bear. They were filled to the top with unresolved pain and tension. Instead of becoming more intimate as they grew older, the coach and his wife each harbored growing resentment for one another. By the time they realized they really needed to face their problems and endure the pain of working through them, they both felt that it was too late. He encouraged us to not make the same mistakes in our relationships.

By not confronting and resolving painful experiences as we encounter them, we not only jeopardize relationships but we undermine our own ability to feel lasting hope and joy. As children, we don't yet have the capacity to understand the importance of learning to consciously endure the pain in life rather than run from it. But, as we grow older, we must come to the conclusion that the only way to really get past emotional pain is to go through it. I know this to be true, having learned by experience.

My doctors and their staff encouraged me to consciously grieve the loss of my leg. I was told it was not only OK to admit my feelings of helplessness, but it was necessary if I was ever to resolve them.

My wife requested that I allow her to help by sharing with her the feelings and incredible pain that this tragedy was causing me. She was in pain as well and needed the support of enduring it together. I had always felt that it was a sign of weakness to admit that I was having trouble handling anything emotionally. I was afraid of becoming more transparent and allowing Pam to see what I perceived as weakness, because I believed it would harm our relationship. I thought that exposing my fears would show her that I was less of a man and therefore not as attractive. Boy, was I wrong. As I began to open up and become more vulnerable to Pam, I discovered how incredibly supportive she could be. We grew closer than ever through our agonizing bouts confronting our sorrow and grief. For the first time in my life, I felt that it was OK to cry in front of her. The level of intimacy in our relationship grew in direct proportion to the amount of transparency that she and I allowed ourselves to share.

When I was finally able to share my feelings, an amazing revelation occurred to me. I learned that by facing the pain, enduring the heartache and sharing the experience with someone safe, I was able to ultimately resolve feelings. It was as if the pain inside of me was hiding in a dark room somewhere deep in my heart. The last thing I wanted to do was open the door to let light in. I was afraid that once the light came in, it would reveal the darkness and expose me to the emptiness that the pain created. If I were forced to recognize and wrestle with the pain, I was afraid I might not win and the horrible darkness would overtake me. The reality of what I discovered was just the opposite. Once the door was open and the light had exposed the pain, it was no longer dark. Instead the room became full of light and only then could I begin to see what needed to be done. I realized it would not destroy me. It lost its sting. Its strength continued to diminish the longer I endured it. Finally, it had no power over me at all. Rather than being shoved into my backpack or repressed deep inside of me, it was out and gone. It had been reduced to a memory that could no longer hurt me.

Having the love and support of my wife to help through the grieving gave me the courage to open my heart and soul to her. With her help, I was able to face and endure the pain once it was exposed. I know I could not have recovered so quickly and moved through this experience so well if I were forced to do it alone.

We all need to cultivate a relationship with at least one person to whom we feel safe enough to become completely transparent. It could be someone we know intimately, a family member, a close friend, or even a therapist. The burden of life becomes lighter when we have someone to whom we can safely expose our deepest hurts and painful experiences. We should also strive to be the kind of person who is willing to support someone else. Everyone needs encouragement to be able to acknowledge, confront, and move through the problems we encounter in life.

It took a great deal of time, effort and support from others to really grasp the positives of what had happened to me. In addition to the growth of the relational intimacy between Pam and me, there were several other rewards. I experienced things such as increased self-esteem and acceptance, unconditional love from my family and friends, and the additional life lessons I learned which were mentioned in chapter two.

After my amputation, I was challenged more than any other time in my life to make the choice to behave as a victim or a victor. It was the biggest single change that I had ever faced. As I was finally able to emerge from the pain, I knew that I wanted to do something special with the rest of my life. Without the heavy baggage of unresolved pain, I had the freedom to look to the next challenges I might face. I was able to start considering the future and deciding once again what I really wanted to be when I grew up. From there, I began to imagine what that was, and a vision began to materialize.

4

DARE TO DREAM

"The foremost obstacle to experiencing success in our lives is our own construction of barriers that paralyze us from taking action."

I have always been a dreamer. As a young child, I imagined and believed that someday I was going to be famous. Born in Tacoma, Washington, in 1959, I lived there until I was three years old and my family moved about 100 miles north to Everett, which was closer to my paternal grandparents. We stayed in Everett for a few years until my grandfather passed away. My father then bought his parents' home from his mother, and we all moved into the same house he grew up in. I was ten years old at the time.

The house was in the small town of Snohomish, Washington, about thirty miles directly north of Seattle. It was a town of about 3,000 people during my youth; it isn't much larger today. No matter where you lived in town you were within walking distance of anything else. It seemed that everyone knew everyone else and all of their business. The town was so small that even if you dialed a wrong number you would probably talk for thirty minutes. Dairy farms and evergreen trees surrounded the area. Best of all, it was a safe and healthy place to raise a family, the two main reasons Pam and I chose to move back after the NFL. We wanted our children to experience that type of small town security. There wasn't much excitement in Snohomish, and you couldn't get into too much trouble unless you really tried. For some typical excitement in the evening you could go down to the river on the edge of town and listen to the old sawmill rust.

As a child, I spent a great deal of time using my active imagination and playing by myself. Not that there wasn't anyone to play with. I had a brother who was one year older than me and we got along pretty well. Also, I had my two younger sisters to pick on, in addition to some neighbor kids who came over occasionally to play. But I enjoyed spending time by myself and dreaming about what the future held.

At different times in my childhood I saw myself growing up to be a rock star, a military hero, or even a professional athlete. I used to stand in front of the mirror in my bedroom strumming an old guitar and playing along with songs on the radio as if it were me singing and playing. I could imagine the girls cheering for me and fainting. After one of my "rock concerts" I could easily change dreams and become a commando. I had seen a movie on television about a World War II Medal of Honor winner. I just knew that someday I could do that. I was a one-man wrecking crew storming our garage with toy guns blazing. I imagined myself wiping out entire armies and receiving a medal of my own. As I grew older and began to participate in sports, I continued to dream. But now I visualized playing in the NBA or NFL. I could play basketball or football in my backyard for hours in front of huge imaginary crowds.

I am not the least bit embarrassed to share these private moments of my childhood because I believe that my dreams were the foundation to my future success. Many, if not all, worthwhile endeavors begin with a dream or a vision. The excitement that the dream creates gives you a reason to jump up in the morning and look forward to the day. Your seemingly unrealistic dream or vision can give you the desire to start plotting a realistic plan to get there through the development of goals. These are activities that can stimulate hope and direction for your life.

Dreaming should come naturally, but the older we get the worse dreamers we seem to become. As an adult, I had the great fortune to relearn what came naturally to me as a child by watching my own children's early years of discovering life. We are hardwired at birth with the capacity to imagine ourselves doing great and wondrous things. The most thrilling aspect of this gift is that whatever we imagine ourselves doing at this young age, we automatically believe completely and instinctively that we can and will accomplish it.

The inspiring rediscovery of this lost childhood ability was and is a great inspiration to me. Rediscovering it, however, can be a shocking experience. Especially if you are reminded of it by your 4-year-old son dressed in his favorite Superman pajamas, complete with cape, standing on the balcony of your home yelling, "Watch me, mommy, I'm going to fly."

I have the opportunity to travel the country and speak with thousands of children and young adults in our nation's schools. One of my favorite questions to ask all age groups is *What are you going to be when you grow up*? I am always fascinated by the vast difference in responses from students in kindergarten to those in middle or high school.

Have you been to a kindergarten room lately? It is certainly invigorating. You may or may not remember those great and exciting first few days of school when you were wearing your new school clothes and carrying that brand new kindergarten box your mom filled with all the required kindergarten stuff. Remember those scissors that really couldn't cut anything, and those crayons that were so fat you could hardly lift them? I finally got curious enough to ask a kindergarten teacher why we were required to buy our children such fat crayons. She looked at me as though I should have already known the answer and very calmly explained, "Well, the children have a much harder time getting the fat ones stuck up their noses." All of a sudden it made perfect sense. Oh, and who could forget the most important item mom packed—the paste, which was great for snacks.

I enjoy opportunities to visit kindergarten classes and ask the children what they want to be when they grow up. Usually, every hand in the room goes up. Kids are bouncing on their chairs, grunting "ooh, ooh" because they want to be called on first. Contrast that with asking that same question in a room full of high school students. Maybe two hands go up. There are probably five or six more who have a pretty good idea of what they might want to do, but they're not going to risk sharing it with the rest of the group for fear of experiencing the pain of disapproval from their peers. Grown-ups can even be worse, saying things like *I'm too old to dream or I'm too busy trying to get through today, much less dream about the future.*

With 5- and 6-year-olds, the experience is somewhat different:
"OK, you in the front. What do you want to be?"
"The president of the United States."
"How about you?" you ask, moving on to the next student. "What is your dream?"
"I'm gonna be a pro football star."
"And you, how about you?" pointing to another child.
"I am going to be the chief of police."
"All right, that's great. Now, how about letting some of the boys answer."
"I'm going to be a fireman," says the first boy.
"I'm going to be the fire chief," says the next, not to be outdone.
"Oh yeah, well I'm gonna be a fire truck!" says the third boy as he starts running around the room, making siren noises.

What a thrill it is to be involved in a scene like this. It is inspirational to recognize the incredible imagination and ability to dream these youth naturally possess. It is a joy to see within these children a confidence that whatever they dream and believe they will most certainly achieve.

What in the world happens to us? Why is it that between kindergarten and the rest of our lives, we somehow lose this awesome belief in our potential and undeniable confidence in our ability to imagine a dream and accomplish it?

Periodically, I watch or listen to a motivational tape. On one occasion, I was viewing a video of a gifted speaker named Rolfe Carawan. During his talk he told a story that I believe gives a very good description of what happens to rob us of our natural ability to believe life will become what we dream it to be. The following is my best attempt to paraphrase his illustration.

Rolfe shared a childhood story that involved his grandmother, who owned a fish tank that was home to an ugly old fish called a wall-eyed pike. I'll give the fish the name "Fred." Every day, Rolfe's grandmother would send him to the pet store with enough money to purchase several guppies to bring home as lunch for old Fred. The young boy enjoyed watching this fat old fish chase and gobble up these unwitting little guppies so much that he would invite the neighbor children to join him during the daily feeding.

One day, on the way home from the pet store, one of the children noticed a piece of Plexiglas lying in the ditch beside the road. This inspired an idea. They brought the Plexiglas home, shined it up, and fashioned it to fit perfectly down the center of the fish tank. The children were then very careful to make sure that the guppies were dropped on the opposite side of the Plexiglas from Fred. As they expected, Fred saw lunch, went for it, and smacked full speed right into the hard Plexiglas. Rolfe described it as one of the funniest things he had ever witnessed. Fred shook his head from side to side, his eyes rolled around a little as he backed up and without a moment's hesitation went after lunch a second time at full speed and crashed face first once again. The children fell to the floor laughing. The fish tried again and again until the giggling children noticed that he had finally stopped. Fred was completely still and would not move. The old fish just stared through the Plexiglas at the free-roaming lunch on the other side of this invisible barrier.

Beginning to get bored with the lack of action, the kids pulled the Plexiglas out of the tank. Much to their surprise the wall-eyed pike did not move; he stayed completely still. The guppies started to swim around, even daring to swim right past the face of old Fred. Rolfe described how you could almost hear the fish saying to himself, *I am so hungry, and you look so delicious. But I am not stupid! I tried to eat you before, and I failed. I tried again, and it hurt. Oh no, I'm not stupid. I will just stay here where it is safe. Even if I have to starve, I'll be satisfied right where I am.* Opportunities were literally inches away, and all Fred had to do was have the courage to try one more time.

I sincerely believe that what happened to the wall-eyed pike in this scenario happens to us, starting as little children and continuing through adulthood. At birth, we received the gift of dreaming and believing. Then we were introduced to failure and experienced pain, or we shared our dreams with someone we cared about and they laughed. Maybe we got the message that what we were proposing was impossible when we heard someone say, "You had better make your goals a little more realistic." It is then that we start to erect this invisible wall to remind us to not go that way again. We believe the wall is necessary to keep us safe from failure and criticism. Often we forget that we have even built the wall, as it becomes so natural to our way of thinking and shields us from pain and disappointment.

The catch is that after we build it, the wall is also very successful at blocking our progression towards anything challenging. Many people wander through life having forgotten the gift of dreaming because they are literally afraid of using it. They refuse to follow the dreams of their youth or dare to create new ones as adults because they are convinced that the result will be painful, and they are not willing to endure it.

You will fail. That is a given. We all do, and it hurts. I can remember games in the NFL when I had a bad day or the opponent was simply better than me and I failed miserably. I not only suffered the pain of failing on game day, but was subjected to the humiliation of watching it over again on film with teammates and coaches. But, like the fish, we must not pass up the next opportunity because we fear the pain that failure brings. One of the coaches with the Raiders, Earl Leggett, had a great saying which encouraged us to not quit. He said in his colorful, deep Louisiana southern drawl, "Boys, sometimes you get the bull and sometimes the bull gets you. Either way you just hop on and ride again." It is only those who have the courage to continue to dream and reach for the opportunities in the face of failure who will experience the joy of achieving their full potential.

This same principle manipulates the largest animal with the most powerful potential in the circus. When an elephant is first brought to the circus, a huge stake is driven in the ground and the elephant's hind leg is chained to it. In its youth and passion the elephant fights and pulls to get away. After a few months of failing to escape and feeling the chain painfully tighten around its skin, the elephant gives up. At that point the trainers no longer have to use the chain. The elephant is controlled by his own belief that he cannot move. The trainer simply pounds a stake in the ground, and the biggest most powerful being in the circus chooses to stand next to the stake. Prior failed attempts have led the elephant to believe it cannot go anywhere.

It is frightening to realize that a disproportionate number of our youths, teenagers and adults in America feel as helpless as the wall-eyed pike and the elephant. Many become consumed by the belief that there is no hope for their future. They feel they could not go anywhere even if they tried. This lack of hope often leads to depression and even death. I recently heard on the radio that suicide is the third leading cause of death among America's 15- to 20-year-olds, and that the suicide rate among children 10 to 14 has doubled since 1980.

We have learned to avoid the pain of failure at all costs. For some, this pain may be caused by valid medical problems, such as a chemical imbalance that leads to depression or anxiety disorders. In these cases, treatment is the answer. However, many are healthy and have just accepted the lie that they are limited in what they can accomplish. They believe it is easier to set no standards for their lives, rather than make the effort to raise them. When there is no hope for the future, all things, including human life, can become insignificant.

As I was recovering from the amputation, I knew from my past experiences that in order to get out of the hole I felt I was in, I needed a challenge. I needed to set a goal to achieve something and start looking forward to what I *could* do, instead of dwelling on what could not be done.

On October 11, 1994, I was released from the hospital after a three-week stay. I recovered at home for another three months before returning to my job with the City of Everett. My recovery involved weeks of therapy, the fitting and development of the prosthesis that would enable me to walk again, and many agonizing hours practicing how to walk with the use of my new artificial leg.

During one of the fittings for my new leg at Cornerstone Prosthetics in Everett, a challenge presented itself. I picked up a magazine in the waiting room that featured amputees who competed in athletic competitions. Some played golf, others track and field, some basketball, volleyball, and many other sports. I thumbed through the pages looking at these athletes competing in regional and national competitions organized by a governing body in charge of putting together a team to represent the United States in the Paralympics held every four years in conjunction with the regular Olympic Games. Like many people, I had never heard of the Paralympics and at first confused them with the Special Olympics. The Special Olympics are competitions for the mentally challenged, whereas the Paralympics are for the physically disabled. The Paralympics include most of the Olympic events and are held in the same venues before or after the regular Olympic Games.

I asked my Prosthetists, Doug and Dave, about these Paralympic competitions. They said they were quite a big deal and offered to sponsor sending me to one if I was interested. The more I thought about the challenge and the opportunity to become an athletic competitor again, the better it began to sound.

After a month of rehabilitation, I started working out on the weight machines at the physical therapy facility. The harder I worked the better I felt, and the more that competitive fire started to burn in my gut. I decided to find out more about these competitions and events in which I might be able to compete. I was pleased to see that power lifting was one of the events. It was actually a very strict form of the bench press. Because you are competing against amputees and wheelchair-bound athletes, the lift required that your legs be extended and strapped to the bench during the lift. This makes it a much more difficult lift because you cannot use your legs for stability or power.

I made the decision that I was going to begin training to compete in the 1995 Wheelchair and Amputee National Championships to be held in Boston that summer. I started to visualize myself winning the Gold Medal in power lifting. This dream gave me the incentive to not just recover but to improve. After a month, the weights at my physical therapist's office were not heavy enough for me, so I bought a membership at a local gym and set out on my quest to become a competitive athlete again. It was a blast. Although it was hard work, it was exciting to be working towards an athletic goal again after six years of being in and out of surgeries. Doug and Dave bought into my enthusiasm and made the commitment to sponsor my trip to Boston.

I set goals, planned workouts, trained hard and got support from those around me. By June I was getting stronger, but nowhere near as strong as I was when I played football. It was getting closer to the competition and I was concerned with how well I would do. By the time I left for Boston I had resolved to just give it my best shot and be satisfied with that.

The competition was great, and I ended up winning the Gold Medal in the power lifting competition. It was refreshing to taste the thrill of competition again, and winning made it that much sweeter. However, after the competition I made the decision not to train for the 1996 Paralympics in Atlanta. I had a job and a family and needed to focus my energies there. Besides, I had started to imagine new areas in which I could challenge myself to improve.

The best experience of the National Championships was having the opportunity to meet and share stories with the other disabled athletes. It was an encouragement to hear their inspirational stories of recovery. All of the athletes were housed in the dormitories on the MIT campus and were crammed in three to a room. After living the high life during my days in the NFL, staying in the best hotels and eating the finest foods, it was quite a shock to be thrust into a setting that was so stark and uncomfortable.

Chuck was one of my roommates. He was in a wheelchair and paralyzed from the waist down. He had been in college when his roommate decided to buy a handgun. Chuck didn't like guns and had cautioned his roommate about the dangers of leaving the gun loaded in the top drawer of the desk they shared in their room. One day Chuck was in a hurry to get to class and he quickly pulled open the desk drawer looking for a pen. The drawer flew open, and as the gun slid forward it went off. The bullet went right through his stomach and lodged in his spinal cord, severing the nerves. One moment the man was getting ready to jog to class and the next he was lying on the floor, a paraplegic. Despite this man's circumstances he had finished college, gotten a job as an engineer, and began competing in table tennis. He had been a two-time national champion.

Not once did I hear Chuck complain. As a matter of fact, he repeatedly told us how lucky he felt he had been. Another few inches and he would have been dead. This man was truly a victor. He said he had dealt with his anger toward his roommate and forgiven him. He had resolved his anger at God and conceded that God had a plan for his life and this was just part of it. Not good, not bad. Just life. He encouraged me to do the same and I was inspired. I wanted to be able to encourage people in the same way that he inspired me.

The most amazing individual that I met during my time at MIT was a young boy named Robert. At the age of 13, he had come all the way from south Florida to compete in two races and weightlifting, even though he could not walk very well. Robert was born with only stumps where his legs should have been, and he was using two very old and damaged artificial legs. In addition to the handicap of his legs, one arm was deformed and all but useless. The only reason

Robert was there was his desire to win a medal. He had attended an assembly at his junior high school where medals were presented to some boys and girls who had competed in a track meet. Robert was so impressed with the medals that he asked his mom if there were any other kids like him, adding that, if so, he would like to race them and get one of those medals. His mother began asking around and found out about the Wheelchair and Amputee National Championships.

I learned from one of the sponsors of the event that Robert and his mother were extremely poor. They had scraped together enough money for the registration fee, but that was it. So, Robert had gone door to door offering to wash cars, mow lawns, and weed flower beds to earn enough money for their bus fare. After all of his hard work and determination just to have a shot at a medal, Robert raced twice and was beaten both times. He competed in weightlifting, despite his deformed arm, but couldn't lift much more than his own body weight. Robert did not win a medal, but neither did he wallow in a cloud of self-pity and disappointment. In fact, as he was leaving, he told us that he would be back next year—bigger, stronger, and faster—and he was going to win himself a medal. If there were medals for bravery and valor in the jaws of adversity, Robert would be wearing several Golds.

Many are never compelled to challenge themselves to dream of being something more than they are right now. They have erected their own depressing invisible shields of past failures that translate to them that their lives are hopeless. They are convinced that things will never change and they must accept their lot in life. They have built these defenses which stop them from even starting to dream. Robert has been running into walls all of his life. After being told he could not do something, he would just try harder. He believed he could achieve his goals regardless of the disappointments of previous failures. If Robert can do it, so can you and I.

I am challenging all of us to remember for ourselves and remind others what incredible gifts we were given when we came into this world. And I urge you to choose to utilize the powerful gifts of dreams and imagination you inherited as a newborn and live the gift of empowerment that working toward your dreams, in spite of past failures, will bring.

The foremost obstacle to experiencing success in our lives is our own construction of barriers that paralyze us from taking action. Although the barriers may be, and most often are conceived in the negative input from others, they can only be erected or dismantled by us. We can truly choose how great we want to be.

Relearning how to dream like a kindergartner is the first step to reaching your potential. Step two is choosing the courageous action of going through your invisible wall and, therefore, obliterating the illusion that it exists at all. The third step includes the setting of goals and the construction of a plan to achieve them. As you progress from step to step, it is essential to realize that every single decision you make will either bring you closer to your dream . . . or take you further away.

5

THE POWER OF DREAMS IN ACTION

"Dreams coupled with goals and subsequent actions always take you somewhere."

As a young boy one of my favorite activities was climbing trees. My grandmother's house had several awesome trees to climb. In one, my grandfather had actually built a very cool tree house in which we played for hours. My favorite trees, however, were the three that were side by side and nearly the exact same size and height. These were great racing trees. I would get my brother, one of my sisters, or a couple of friends, and we would race. We would all begin at the bottom of a tree with the goal of getting to the top first. Someone would yell *Go*! and the first to the top was declared the winner. Some of us were better than others and won more often. The winner was not necessarily the most nimble at climbing trees.

As you read earlier, I am 6 feet, 5 inches tall, weigh over 350 pounds, and have never experienced a growth spurt in my life. I have always been huge. I was the tallest and biggest in my kindergarten class and every class after that through my senior year in high school. Shoot, I was born big; my father had to run out and buy cigars that proclaimed *It's a man*! So one could conclude that at my size, I certainly wasn't the fastest tree climber in the world. Yet, I won many tree races. I had learned early that the more time I spent studying the trees, looking at the branches and planning ahead which ones would get me to the top the quickest and safest, the better my advantage over the person who just started up the tree with no plan at all.

In preparing to reach my goal of getting to the top of the tree first, I would look for the thick, sturdy, safe limbs that were close enough to each other for quick climbing. The good limbs were always surrounded by those that looked easier and more tempting to grab. Those limbs were either too thin to hold me or weakened by rotting and cracking. To grab on to one of those tempting, easier limbs for support would be a guaranteed quick trip back to where I started. With the best branches scouted out, I would be able to make quicker and more reliable decisions about which branches to grab. The better decisions I made in the shortest amount of time led me to my quest for success in reaching the top first.

Having goals in life, just like the goal of getting to the top of the tree, is required for success. But dreaming, in and of itself, is not enough. The dream is the mechanism that propels you to develop the goals and then the plan to achieve those goals. The more thorough the plan, the easier it becomes to make the quick but reliable decisions in life that lead you in the direction of achieving your dream.

Developing the dream provides a beginning point for a plan. The plan is the arranging of the goals or steps you will take to get you where you say you want to go. Your dream and subsequent plan should inspire you to take the time to consider the best choices when options present themselves. Having a goal will help direct your decisions by giving you the opportunity to test a proposed action by asking yourself one question: *Will the action I am about to take produce the desired outcome to help me achieve my goals and eventually my dream*?

Dreams also have a way of evolving as you move through life learning from the experience each decision brings. Many times dreams will transform into new and exciting possibilities for your life. For example, when I was young, my dream was to be a professional basketball player. I went to camps, and practiced developing my athletic capabilities such as quick hands and feet. I worked extremely hard on my leg strength and explosion in order to be able to dunk the basketball. Every chance I got I would go to my backyard hoop and challenge an imaginary NBA star such as Dr. J or Wilt Chamberlain, the Michael Jordan and Shaquille O'Neal of my day, to a game of one on one. In these games I was an NBA star, as well as a play-by-play commentator. The games usually ended with me, as the commentator, describing a thrilling, last-second shot by Curt Marsh as I swished a jump shot.

When I got into high school my body quit growing taller and started to grow wider. That's when, although still playing and loving basketball, I took the opportunity to try out for the football team before my sophomore year in high school. All of the work I had done preparing myself to be a great NBA star had helped me to acquire physical skills that were uncommon for a young man of my size. My well-developed quickness, foot and hand speed, as well as leg strength and explosion, were great assets to my ability to ultimately perform and succeed in football. Had I not had that dream and goal to be an NBA star and had not worked so hard to achieve that dream, I would not have developed the physical attributes that catapulted me to stardom later in football.

Dreams take you somewhere. Not always where you planned to go, but with a dream and a working plan to achieve that dream you could end up succeeding in many different areas of your life. It is because of this belief that I am excited that all of my children have their own dreams and are working toward them. It gives them a structure for their decisions and a hope for their future.

My oldest son, Jake, is 17 and built much like I am. He is 6 feet,

4 inches tall and a solid 275 pounds. As a result, many assume he may have aspirations of following in dad's footsteps and playing football. Jake receives a great deal of pressure to play and has considered it. He is a strong, agile kid who did quite well when he played basketball. But he has other talents and dreams. I learned this for the first time when Jake was about 4 years old. He handed me a drawing he had just finished, and I looked at it and asked which book he had traced it from. It was such an incredible likeness of the cartoon character it depicted. He looked at me with a scowl and said, "I didn't trace it. I drew it!" I was astounded by his talent and told him so. I then asked if he had considered being an artist when he grew up. By his reaction to that question, I knew I had said something to offend him. He looked me right in the eye and said, "Father, I *am* an artist!" and stomped out of the room. I knew right then and there that he was right. My son is now an extremely accomplished singer/songwriter and has recorded his first demo CD. He is truly gifted in the areas of music and art, and his dream is to be a successful recording artist. My wife and I have worked hard to support him because we know that his dreams will take him somewhere.

My other son, Christopher (I call him CJ), has a completely different physical makeup than his older brother. CJ is 15 years old, about 6 feet tall, and weighs in at a whopping 160 pounds. Guess what his dream is to be. You got it, a professional football player. Go figure. I've got one son you could possibly land a plane on and another one who used to have to run around in the shower to get wet, and it seems as though their dreams and their bodies don't necessarily match. It really doesn't matter how big CJ is, however, because it's what he does with his dreams that makes him powerful.

CJ's interest in athletics was noticed at a very young age. By the age of two, he could identify the city and name of each NFL team simply by seeing their helmet. He already had a favorite NFL player by the age of three, and it wasn't me. For birthdays and Christmas, his number one request was always for one of those tiny tot NFL team uniforms available in the larger catalogue stores. He also had to have football cleats "like the real guys wear." He was so into football as a toddler that I began to get a little concerned that he might be too focused on one thing at such an early age.

My concern hit its peak when the whole family was moving back to Washington from California for the last time in 1987. We had rented a large U-Haul truck to move our furniture and other belongings. The truck only had two seats up front, but it had a little sliding door behind the seats that opened up the cargo area. We put our dining room table in the truck first and pushed it right up next to the sliding door. Then we packed everything else around it, leaving the area under the table for our two boys Jake, age five, and CJ, three years old. We arranged cushions, blankets and pillows so they would have a comfortable area in which to sleep or play during our long drive home.

When it started to get dark on the first night, Pam and I could hear the boys behind us talking about the movie *The Wizard of Oz*, which we had seen the night before. CJ's voice was thick with concern when I heard him say to his brother, "There aren't any real witches, with real powers, like that one in the movie. Are there, Jacob?" Jake responded by saying, "No, Christopher. There aren't." But in true big brother fashion, he immediately followed up with a big growl and, "But there are demons!" CJ shot up to the front like he had been fired from a cannon yelling, "Mommy! Mommy! Are there really demons? Jacob said there are demons." Before answering she gave Jake that look that mothers have which communicates disapproval without saying a word. She then looked down at CJ as he clutched her leg. Not wanting to lie to him, and considering her spiritual beliefs, she said in a very calm, reassuring tone, "Yes, CJ, there are demons. But you don't have to worry about them or be afraid, because God already beat them and he protects you." CJ loosened his grip as he looked up at mommy, believing her, and said, "That's right, mommy. God's the biggestest and strongestest ever. Isn't he, mommy?" She replied, "Yes." CJ added, "He can beat anyone. Can't he, mommy?" "Yes," she replied. Suddenly his whole face lit up as though he had come to some incredible revelation. He then turned to me, and in an enthusiastic, heartfelt voice he asked, "Dad, does God play football?" That's when I really got concerned with little CJ's priorities.

CJ has grown to be a very gifted athlete with a strong will and a stubborn work ethic. Regardless of how big CJ grows to be, I have no doubt he is capable of achieving his dream. Because dreams coupled with goals and subsequent actions always take you somewhere.

My daughter, Jillian Rose Marsh, is 10 years old and currently the President & CEO of the Marsh family. For those of you who have experienced or are experiencing this "youngest child who rules without anyone realizing it syndrome," you know exactly what I am talking about. The worst part is that she has daddy wrapped around her little finger, and she knows it. She brags to anyone who will listen that she's daddy's girl and spoiled rotten. It is not my intent to spoil her or let her rule the home. It just seems to be this supernatural force that she has over me. The force is her uncanny ability to connect with that soft spot deep inside of me and then, without conscience, manipulate it.

One such manipulation occurred a couple of years ago. Jillian and I had spent some time together on a Sunday watching pro football, including all the commercials. One popular beer commercial had a guy in possession of his last Bud Light. His friend wanted it so badly, that he was willing to grovel to get it. In a last attempt to get his friend to share, the guy hugs his friend and with tears in his eyes tells him how much he loves him. The friend is moved, but he still won't give up the beer. That night when it was bedtime, I was

Me (#77 jumping) in a high school championship game during my senior year at Snohomish High School.

Coach Jim Lambright, my father Hugh, and me signing a letter of intent to go to The University of Washington to play football.

At The University of Washington, in 1980, I was honored with the Rising Award (Offensive Lineman of the Year). I played in the 1978 Rose Bowl, 1979 Sun Bowl, 1981 Rose Bowl, East West Shrine Game and the Japan Bowl.

I was the first-round draft choice of the Raiders and the first rookie to start on the offensive line since Gene Upshaw in 1967.

(photo above) me (#60),
leading the way for
Marcus Allen (#32)
& Jim Plunkett (#16).

1986 photo of my
first-born son, Jake, and me.

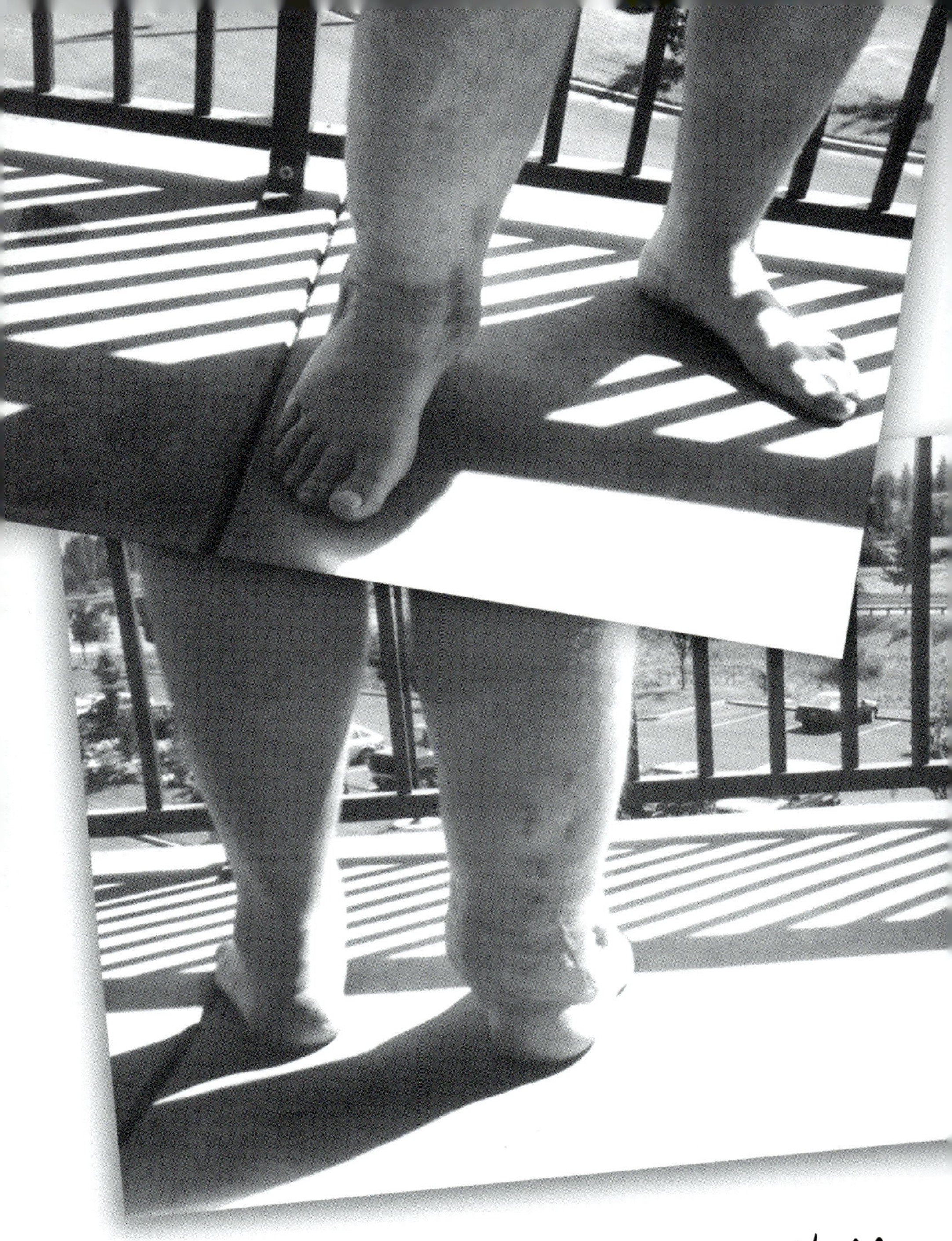

Due to the accumulation of football injuries, this is what my ankle looked like before the amputation in 1994. I was not very far from "Rock Bottom."

(photo above) My wife Pam, my daughter Jillian, and me at home just one month after the amputation.

These are my three wonderful children— Jillian, Jake and Christopher.

Here I am training for and winning the Gold Medal in power lifting during the 1995 Wheelchair & Amputee Championships.

tucking Jillian in and she started telling me the reasons she shouldn't have to go to bed yet. First it was that she was thirsty, then it was the bathroom trip and so on. Finally, I put my foot down and told her there was absolutely nothing she could say or do to convince me to let her out of bed again. At that moment she looked at me with those puppy dog eyes and said, "Daddy, I can't go to sleep yet. I have to call grandpa and tell him just how much I love him." This warmed my heart, and I could not help but give in. I actually dialed the phone for her. When I handed her the phone, she told grandpa that she loved him so much. Then right away she asked, "Grandpa, do you love me?" It was so cute. I'm sure my father went on for a while describing his love for her until Jillian gave me a glance that let me know something was up. The phone came away from her ear just far enough for me to hear grandpa telling her that he loved her more than any other girl in the whole wide world. This brought a big smile to her face and then the response, "You know, grandpa, that's great. But guess what? You're still not getting my Bud Light!" She was repeating the punch line of the beer commercial we had seen at least a dozen times while watching football earlier that day. She giggled and hung up the phone. I felt so used. I said nothing and just pointed towards her room, trying hard to be stern and not laugh. She trotted off to bed, just happy knowing she still had daddy right where she wanted him.

Jillian's dream is to be a teacher. My bet is that it won't be long before she's the principal. I know she has what it takes to accomplish a life full of success.

In addition to their personal goals, each of our children is subject to some family goals regarding home and school. It is thrilling to see them setting goals and making decisions in their lives based on the bigger dream they have. Every chance we get, Pam and I encourage them by reminding them of the goals and plans they have shared, and urge them to wade through the failures or setbacks by adjusting their plans to achieve their goals.

My own dreams are evolving, and the subsequent goals I set and plans I make to achieve them must be constantly adjusted. As I grew through the amputation experience, my vision or dreams for my own life became more focused and passionate. My career goal, after my experiences with football and the vending business, was to make a living and support my family by doing something I felt passionate about and enjoyed doing. I found that opportunity at the City of Everett, working with and for the youth in my community.

By 1995, I had been working with high-risk youth for five years. We had developed and implemented programs focusing on gang-involved youth, as well as street youth and runaways. Many children were helped. However, the human service and recreation systems in Everett and the surrounding region were becoming increasingly burdened with disenfranchised youth who had no hope for their future.

That's when I began to create a new vision for my professional life. I knew I wanted to continue to positively affect youth, and I felt motivated to find new opportunities to communicate to greater numbers of kids the reality that they are unique and special. In addition, I also wanted to find ways to share what I knew to be true with adults. Thus, I began working toward the goal of speaking full-time. It is a pleasure to share with people everywhere that there is great joy, excitement and purpose that can be found in realizing that you have the power to choose to live successfully. As my understanding of the need grows, so does my vision to reach people in my own small way.

I am committed to the vision of sharing with as many young people and adults as possible, the lessons my life's experiences have taught me. My plan is to use numerous tools to passionately share some of my life's struggles and victories in very real ways. This book, which I hope will be one of many, is one of those tools. I have already spoken to thousands across the country and am looking for ways to reach thousands more with a message of hope. I sincerely believe that I can and will encourage many to recognize and begin to experience their potential for a truly rewarding life, despite their current circumstances.

It all starts with the dream. Dreams are the destination; the goals and plans are the map; the decisions and actions are the steps you take to stay on course. On your journey to your dream, you must have the courage to make the right decisions, even during the hardest of times. For it will ultimately be your choices that affect how quickly you get there.

6

TRUE TOUGHNESS

"True courage and toughness are simply the ability to confront life's experiences while maintaining the integrity of saying and doing what you know to be right in your heart . . . "

Who is the toughest person you know? Depending on your age and your life experiences, a certain person or personality type may come to mind. When I ask this rhetorical question during a high school or middle school assembly, I don't actually have anyone answer. However, it has been my experience from talking to students individually after the assemblies that the response is generally the same. The tough-acting guy or girl with whom no one would want to pick a fight is the person most students think of first. It is then my job to explain what I mean by toughness by asking *What is true toughness*?

Many students seem surprised when I explain to them that in my life's experience with tough guys, and in the NFL you see all kinds, the toughest were those who never bragged about it, never had to prove it, and never had to threaten. Students seem even more surprised when I explain that the people who are always acting tough and doing things to prove it are actually those who usually feel weakest. They hide their weaknesses by acting tough. The same is true for those who feel the need to always act or be cool. Students who must belong to groups of people or cliques that become exclusive and keep others out, because of their appearance or actions, are actually afraid of rejection themselves. The act of rejecting others gives them the illusion of power over their own fears.

The truth is everyone has pain, and everyone fears. As a matter of fact, the very actions someone takes to prove to everyone either how tough or cool they are, is evidence of how afraid they must really feel. In order to hide their fears and weaknesses they must act in such a way as to camouflage and protect their secrets. That is not real toughness or coolness. People who behave in this way are worthy of our concern and efforts to help them find healthy ways to cope with their fear and pain.

The sad fact is that in our schools and our entire culture, those acting the part the best are usually able to convince us that they have no problems and should be admired. When we believe this, we begin to ask ourselves questions like *What's wrong with me*? *Why can't I be more like they are*? And we begin to feel uniquely inadequate. This is not just a teen phenomenon; feelings of inadequacy are rampant in our entire society.

As an example, let's consider the influence of television. When analyzing the goals and accomplishments of television or considering why it is so successful, the conclusion can only be one thing: Television makes money! Lots and lots of money. This money comes from advertisers who buy time on television to sell their products. The main job of anyone who advertises on television is to find the best way to convince us that we, the viewing public, need their product, that we are somehow inadequate and unacceptable to society unless we have what they are offering. And guess what? These people are really good at it. Advertisers have very highly paid staffs of brilliant people working around the clock to design new and improved ways of accomplishing this task.

Now I ask you, what is one of the things that television is successfully doing to our young and old minds day after day? If you were honest you would agree that television has been very successful at convincing millions of Americans, young and old, that they are totally and completely inadequate.

It is no wonder we are concerned with what other people think. We are bombarded daily with messages telling us we need to "fit in" or "keep up." And not just on television. We see the "proof" of our inadequacies on billboards, buses, and buildings. We hear it on the radio. We may even encounter such messages from others who view us or treat us differently if we don't wear the "right" things or own the "right" stuff.

The difficulties come because human beings are so concerned with what everyone else thinks that we choose to make important decisions based on constantly moving and very shaky foundations.

I was driving down the road one day with the radio on, switching stations, and just happened to stop on a station that was reporting on a recent study that was conducted with 10,000 high school students from all over the nation. As I describe the story to you, try to imagine you are the student they have picked from your area to attend this test.

The sponsoring university flies everyone to New York. The first meeting is held with all 10,000 kids in a huge auditorium. You are with 9,999 kids you have never met. The leader explains that they have brought you here for a study that requires answering a couple of questions in small groups. Several adults assist with breaking students up into groups of ten.

You are taken to a sectioned-off area and are now sitting next to nine kids you have never met, with no idea of what you are about to be asked to do. In front of the room there is a large white board. The instructor enters the room and writes the letters A and B about six inches apart from each other at the top of the board. Then directly under each letter he draws a vertical line. The line under the letter A is about three inches long, and the one under the B is drawn all the way to the bottom of the board, about four feet long. The instructor begins to hand out sheets that spell out the same instructions he is about to give. He states that this test is simple. He will point to letter A or B and then ask you to raise your hand if you believe he is pointing to the letter with the longest line under it. He instructs you to not make a sound but just raise your hand when he points to the longest line. The instructor then announces that all of the students will be separated for a few moments and then brought back to take the test.

Imagining myself being escorted to a private waiting area, I know I would be thinking that this is going to be the easiest test I have ever taken in my life. However, if you are the "test student," what you do not know is that the instructor took the other nine students from your group and put them in a room together. He explained to them that excluding *you* is part of the test. He further explained that when they reconvened in the test room, he would point to letter A (the shortest line) and ask everyone who believes it represents the longest line to raise their hand. And here's the twist: He actually wants these nine participants to raise their hands when he points to letter A, even though it has the shorter line. He said the goal is to see how the "test student" will react in the face of peer pressure.

Finally, you are asked to go back in the room. You assume everyone else was alone like you were. The instructor gets to the front and points to the letter A, which has the three-inch line under it, and says, "How many of you believe the letter A has the longest line under it? If so, raise your hand." The other nine students in your group very quickly and confidently raise their hands. I don't know about you, but I know my first thought would be *Now I know I'm in the wrong group. What are the chances that out of 10,000 kids selected from all over the United States I would get stuck with nine stupid ones? Come on, they are wrong!* Then I would probably wonder about the chances of all of them being wrong, or I would start questioning whether I had missed some part of the instructions. Either way, they were all waiting for me.

What would you have done in that situation? I hope I would have done the right thing and had the courage to stick with what I believed to be the right answer. It was very frightening when the announcer on the radio stated that over 75 percent of the test students raised their hands. They were under so much self-inflicted pressure to conform that they lacked the courage of their own convictions, even when they knew they were right.

This study of our students reflects a problem facing people of all ages in our society—one that contributes to our feelings of helplessness and hopelessness. When people live their lives looking for everyone else's reaction or approval only, they lose control of their own decisions, and the power of their dreams is greatly diminished. If we establish a decision-making foundation based on what we think other people might think, we must ask ourselves *Where do* **my** *dreams come in, and who really has control of my life?* Contrast that with the establishment of a decision-making foundation based on what you know is right for you and the goals you have established for your life. Now who has the control of your life's decisions?

It always gives me great pleasure to expose the truth about toughness and courage. We were all born with the ability to be truly courageous and tough. In the school setting it can be the biggest male athlete or the youngest girl. It can be teachers or staff members. In society it can be any one of us.

True courage and toughness are simply the ability to confront life's experiences while maintaining the integrity of saying and doing what you know to be right in your heart, regardless of what anyone else says or thinks about you.

I believe that all but a few are born with a conscience. The great majority of us have a built-in ability to know right from wrong. A friend of mine, Cliff Gillies, who is part American Indian, describes this ability using a legend passed down from his ancestors. The legend says that each of us is born with an invisible triangle in our stomach; its purpose is to keep us from doing that which is wrong. The points of the triangle are sharp and when we begin to think of doing something that is wrong, the triangle begins to spin, creating an uncomfortable turning in our gut. The legend teaches that if you feel this turning in your stomach and choose to stop, the triangle will quit turning and the points will remain sharp and continue to work properly. But if you feel the turning in your gut and keep on doing what you know is wrong, the triangle will keep turning. Over time, if you choose to continue doing that which is wrong, the points on your triangle begin to wear down and discerning right from wrong becomes increasingly difficult. If you continue this too long, you grow to be a person without a triangle at all and can be trusted by no one.

It takes great courage to say and do things simply because they are the right thing to do. Many times we are faced with extremely tough decisions which mean doing right may cause some pain by alienating you from others who disagree with your decisions. All of us want to be accepted and loved. The reality is that we can never please everyone. When you look in the mirror and are proud and satisfied with the integrity of the choices you have made, I guarantee you that there are others who will accept and respect you as well.

7

CONSISTENT COURAGE

"Your courage may have a positive effect on people around you who wanted to take a step but didn't have the strength to do it alone."

In addition to the pressure to make good decisions from the start, it is also difficult to change the foundation from which you have made your decisions in the past. As you establish that new foundation and begin to behave differently because of your courageous decisions, people will notice. If you truly start following your dream, plan to accomplish it, and begin making decisions for the right reasons, your entire life will start to change.

As I stated in previous chapters, change is hard to deal with when it happens to you. Change is also tough to deal with for the people around you, especially when they begin to notice that you are not the same person you were before. Even if the changes are great, exciting and healthy for you, it may be scary for your peers.

I'll share a story to help illustrate what I'm talking about. If you are a water skier, you know the things that I am about to say are true. If you have seen someone water ski and you would like to try some day, it is very important that you pay attention to this part of the book. There are three things that happen to a first-time water skier. I do not care where you learn or who you are with; these three things are fundamental and unavoidable for first-time water skiers.

The first time you try to ski, your friends, who have already helped you put on your life jacket and skis, throw a rope to you as you are floating in the water. The rope you have been thrown is attached to a boat with a big motor. After you have a secure handle on the rope, the instructions are usually something like *Don't worry . . . it's easy . . . just say "hit it."* You say the magic words, and the next thing you know you have let go of the rope that has dragged you 300 yards head-first through the water, forcing you to drink half of the lake. The boat circles around, and only after you let loose with a couple of huge burps are you able to speak. This is usually a great time to ask for some more specific instructions on how to actually get the skis to the surface of the water. After this you are a little bloated and uncomfortable, but you can go on.

The second unavoidable situation occurs when you are finally able to get up on the skis and glide across the water. It is at this time that you are guaranteed to assume the patented first-time water skier position. There is no textbook that can show you how to look this stupid; it just happens automatically. Your legs are fighting to go in opposite directions. Your butt is sticking out and going from side to side as your gut full of lake water is sloshing back and forth. Your arms are extending and recoiling at different times, and you have this stupid grin on your face that comes from only God knows where. I don't care how cool you think you look right now, you are going to look like an idiot and there is nothing you can do about it. At this point you can anticipate a blessing and a curse. The blessing is that this stage won't last very long. The curse is the third and final inevitable catastrophe.

Just as you start to feel pretty good and are beginning to look like a real water skier, you will be allowed to go about another 100 yards. And then it happens. Regardless of whom you are with or even if your sweet grandmother is driving the boat, at the precise moment you reach 100 yards a conspiracy begins to brew. Your "friends" in the boat will turn to each other with a wicked smile and, in unison, say, "Now, let's whip 'em in a circle!" Whip, indeed. In this situation, you will be convinced you have achieved Mach 2 on the water's surface. And when you are going that fast, lots of things start happening. Have you ever stuck your head out of the car window on the freeway? You'll start that breathing thing, where your mouth is wide open but no air can get to your lungs. The next thing you notice is the bugs hitting you in the forehead and you start to duck because they feel and sound as though they must be bullets. Then you are back to the breathing thing. With your mouth wide open, other bugs are shooting down your throat. The human body's digestive system works incredibly fast at Mach 2. It's amazing.

Now here comes the worst part. When a human body is doing Mach 2 on water skis and falls, it skips like a smooth stone across a still pond. I'm not making this up. But beware: Your swimsuit will not skip with you. I know this because it happened to me. There I was, thinking I was finally looking good, and the next thing I know I am twenty feet below the surface with my trunks around my ankles praying for little things like air and light. I just wanted to live. Immediately, I start thinking and realized I would get to the top a lot faster if I could kick. So I bent over to start pulling my trunks up from around my ankles. I am completely doubled over working on this for some time when I'm sure you can guess which part of my anatomy happens to float to the surface first. Now I have a whole new set of problems. I have to worry about people with harpoons. And there just happens to be a member of Greenpeace on the lake shouting to everyone through a megaphone, "Get back. Get back. Save the whale!" Little kids are grabbing at their parents, yelling, "Look, they freed Willy!"

Obviously I am stuck in a terrible situation. The moment I realize what is going on I think to myself—my buddies! Those friends of mine still in the boat. Surely they will dive in and risk their lives to save me. Fat chance! They were "busting a gut" laughing so hard. But they were not just laughing; they also started verbally abusing me. "You suck!" they shouted. "You're the worst water skier on the lake." Turning to the onlookers, they yelled, "We don't even know him. We picked him up on shore." Then they were back to me, begging me not to fall again for fear I would empty the lake. It was horrible.

Later, I realized something about that experience. None of the other guys on the boat had ever water skied either. Not one of them had even tried it. We had borrowed my brother's boat that day and sat out in the middle of the lake for an hour arguing over who was going to try it first. In the end, the others had agreed that since it was my brother's boat, and because I'm big and wouldn't get hurt, I should go first. As I was trying to muster the courage to jump in, I saw a guy glide by on one ski and it looked so cool. "I'm going to learn to ski today," I said to myself. And I jumped out of the boat.

I learned a very powerful lesson that day about how peers react to one of their own taking a courageous step forward. I made a difficult decision to try to achieve something and then backed my decision up with action, and it frightened them. They watched me try to ski and observed how hard it really was. They were scared that if I were successful, they might be expected to do more than just talk about it. In reality their reaction to my courage was no different than how many of your peers may react as you begin to change your life through your actions to achieve your dream. You will be making decisions to behave differently or prioritize your life in ways other than what they are used to. That's when they may do or say things to purposely discourage you in their effort to bring you back to where they are. Back behind the wall where it is safer and easier. If they are successful at getting you to quit, it takes the daunting pressure off them to be courageous too.

I share this with you so you will be prepared to encounter a negative reaction to your positive steps. However, often times the opposite occurs. Your courage may have a positive effect on people around you who wanted to take a step but didn't have the strength to do it alone. You can model courage by your choices and actually lead others to do the same. I've always believed that the most effective leaders are the ones that lead by example.

Taking the water ski example one step further, I had a choice. I could give up and get back in the boat with the others, where I would be comfortable and safe, or I could be courageous and continue to work to improve my abilities by making myself vulnerable to possible failure. By giving up and returning to the safety of the boat I would surely protect myself from future pain. However, I would be no closer to my goal of water skiing than I was when I started. As a matter of fact, once I had tried and then quit, I would probably never try again.

If we think for a moment, I am sure we can all identify someone who has spent most of their life in the safety of the boat. At my 20-year high school reunion I saw people I had not seen or heard from in years. It was interesting to listen to their stories and hear what was important to them. I found that there were some who seemed as though they had not progressed on to anything that challenged them past graduation. These were the folks who talked about high school as though it were the highlight of their life. They had apparently not been able to either step out of the safety of the boats in their life or find the courage to stay out once the swimming got difficult. When we come to those moments in our life that challenge us to make a decision to step out or stay in, we must make the decision that we believe will be right for us based on our dreams and goals for the future.

As my vision for public speaking began to come into reality, I had to make some tough choices. Following my surgery and recovery

I had continued to work for the City of Everett in a very demanding job. While still working, I gradually increased my public speaking engagements and moved closer and closer to the point where I would have to make the leap of faith and quit my job to pursue speaking full-time. When I discussed my plans with others, many of my peers thought I was not making a wise choice. I was making a very comfortable living and had great medical benefits, and they felt it was foolish to throw that away on a venture which may or may not be successful. Because I was the breadwinner of our family, I had many pressures and responsibilities to consider. In the final analysis, I knew what the right decision was for me and my family. I wrote my letter of resignation and followed my passion, my dream, and my plan to do what I am doing now. In retrospect, I could not be more satisfied. My wife and I have been very successful in our venture, and I am able to enjoy both the financial and emotional fulfillment I receive through my efforts.

Believe me when I tell you that making such a change is not always easy. However, doing what I love to do is worth the aggravation that the difficult times bring. My wife and family believe in what we are doing, and we look to each other for strength when times are tough. Because we continue to go through growing pains, it has been important for us to recognize that the people with whom we spend our time always influence our success. None of us, even the strongest, can succeed alone. If you are committed to your dreams, plans, and decisions, you must learn to surround yourself with encouragers rather than discouragers. Encouragers are peers and others who will support your hopes and dreams with more than just words. They are the support we all need to hold us up when we are weak or to keep us going when we want to quit.

8

SURROUND YOURSELF WITH WINNERS

"Surround yourself with people you know will be encouragers in your life . . . not discouragers."

Zion Lutheran School was my educational home from kindergarten through the ninth grade. I grew up in a Christian home and attended the same school my father did when he was young. In my ninth grade year, the entire enrollment in all grades was 205 students; we only had nine kids in my ninth grade class. Needless to say we were not an athletic powerhouse and certainly did not have a football program. That didn't bother me at the time because I was so into basketball. We had a good basketball team and competed against other small Christian schools within about a 100-mile radius.

Our campus was the first floor of the church and the surrounding parking lot. We had more classrooms in an additional building next to the church called the Parish Hall. It was in this building that we had one basketball hoop for practices, stuck at the end of a huge meeting room. For our physical education classes, we would walk about a half mile to the Snohomish Junior High and use its fields for soccer, baseball, and flag football.

The Snohomish Junior High football team was the most feared team in their league and undefeated. Our class time happened to coincide with the time that the football team was about to begin their daily practices. In the ninth grade I was approximately 6 feet, 3 inches tall and 240 pounds, and I'll never forget the laughs and jeers I heard as they walked past us to take the field. They would say things to me like, "Hey, big guy. What's the matter? You not tough enough for real football? Afraid we might hurt you? You guys from Zion will only play with girls." After a while these comments started to make me extremely angry. I knew I couldn't do or say anything to them at the time because the punishment I would get for making Zion School and my parents look bad would be even worse. So I just started memorizing faces and vowed that when I got to Snohomish High the next year, I was going to turn out for football and crush those guys.

Sign-up day approached and I was ready for my sophomore year and football. I reported to the locker room and found out I was one day late. The coach took one look at me and said, "No problem, son. The gear is a bit picked over, but you can play. If I have to go out and buy more gear, you will play." I had grown a little over the summer and with just a couple of days until my 15th birthday, I was already 6 feet, 4 inches tall and 250 pounds—a high school football coach's dream. I didn't have the courage to tell anyone I had never played before. Or that I had never picked out football gear before. The coach was more than happy to try to find me the best stuff left. I got this old helmet that looked a little different than all the others. It had leather inside instead of air and water pockets, and the insignia on the outside was a picture of Snohomish High's panther mascot, rather than just an S. It looked old and it stunk. But I didn't care. I took one look at that hard-shelled apparatus and thought to myself, *I'm gonna crush one of those guys with this thing.*

I was taken to the thigh pads. These are the pads that protect the thigh muscle from bruises. When I played in the NFL my thigh pads were oval, thin, light, and about 6 inches across to allow me to move quickly. The pads my coach handed me were huge. They were not round or oval; they looked more like a rectangle with the top cut off at a 45-degree angle. The top of the wing-like pad had one point higher than the other which, as I think back, was probably so the pad could conform from the groin area up to the outer thigh and hip. These were the pads no one else wanted. But, I didn't care. I thought, *I could crush one of those guys with these things*. I collected all of my equipment into the bag I was provided and was ready for my first practice the following day.

I dragged my equipment bag upstairs and went to bed early. My mom asked if I wanted to stay up a little later, and I replied, "No, mom. I need my rest. I'm crushing people tomorrow." I got up early the next morning. On the way out the door, dragging my equipment behind me, I was asked if I wanted some breakfast. My response was, "No, mom. I haven't got time. I'm on my way to crush people today."

I showed up at the gym, and went to the locker room. I made my entrance. As I walked down the stairs, I looked into the faces of those who had made fun of me the year before, and I knew they were about to be crushed. I took my place in front of my locker, emptied my bag and began to get ready. It wasn't until that point that I realized I had never seen or been told how to put on a football uniform. The average person would not believe the amount of body parts one is required to cover with padding. I had just made my big entrance and was not about to lean to the guy next to me and ask, *Hey, where does this go*? So I started with the obvious. I picked up my helmet, set it on my head, and pushed on the top until it popped on. I then chose the shoulder pads and tried putting them on over my helmet. When I found this to be impossible, I knew I had to take my helmet off and start over. As I squeezed the helmet off of my head, it hurt so much that I thought I had actually ripped my ears off. (Just a side note: If you ever try on a football helmet, be aware that those little holes on the sides are not so you can hear better. Those are to put your fingers in and pull the helmet apart, so when you remove it you do not rip your ears off.) I got my helmet off, quickly checked it for my ears, and then started the whole process again.

I finally managed to get dressed and run onto the field. The coach took one look at me and announced, "Marsh, you are going to be a lineman." I thought, "No kidding." I ran to where the line was and there they were, the guys who had made fun of me. The coach had us line up side by side and face him. The instructions were that the first thing a lineman must have to beat the opponent is a strong foundation. So they were going to teach us the proper three-point stance. (That's the one you see on television where all the fat guys up front with numbers in the 60's and 70's bend over and rest one hand on the ground.) First, we were told to put our feet shoulder-width apart. I did that. We were next instructed to crouch down and rest our elbows on our knees. I did that as well, but it seemed a little tougher. Then we were asked to put one hand on the ground. I reached for the ground as hard as I could but the pain would not let me get close enough to touch. I looked down the line and everyone else had easily put their hand on the ground. I tried again with no success.

This was a great opportunity for the coach to make an example of the new guy. He walked over and said, "The rest of you guys stay down. Hey, Marsh! Put your hand on the ground." I tried again with no luck. He repeated his instructions, and I made one last attempt against the pain. As I bent over, the coach pushed on my back, forcing my hand to the ground. I immediately screamed in agony and jumped up as high and quickly as I could. The coach then got in my face and asked in a stern and surprisingly motivational tone, "Marsh, with flexibility like that, how do you ever expect to become a football player?" I replied, "Coach, it's not my flexibility. Usually this would be very simple for me, but there is something wrong with this uniform." Thinking I was just making an excuse, he grabbed me and said, "OK, let's make an inspection." It didn't take long to find the problem. Remember the thigh pads I received the day before, the ones with the huge wings to protect the outside of my thighs with the point to cover my hip? I had put the high, winged points on the inside. So the lower I got the more they pinched in a very uncomfortable area. When the coach pushed on my back I felt as though my world was coming to an end. Boy, that hurt. The most embarrassing thing was I also sang in the choir and had to be a soprano for two weeks.

This incident was not the most humiliating thing that happened to me that day. The worst thing was that I did not crush anyone. As a matter of fact, it felt like everyone was taking turns crushing me. I did not realize that there was so much skill and technique involved in playing the game of football. I struggled to learn the proper footwork to keep on balance. I couldn't seem to maintain a lower leverage point at all times, and in football the person that is lowest on impact usually wins. It was a horrible experience and extremely humbling.

The whole sophomore season was tough. Since I was the biggest player on the field, everyone thought I must be the best. After the games got underway, people half my size were winning physical battles with me just because they understood the techniques of the game. It was embarrassing and frustrating.

After a season filled with disappointment, football was finally over and basketball season arrived. I was so relieved to play a sport that I knew I was pretty good at. I had been one of the best players in the league when I was at Zion. I wanted to earn a varsity letter as a sophomore my first year at Snohomish. I shared my goal with my mother. In an effort to spare me from having to feel too much disappointment, she told me not to get my hopes up. She said that at Zion I was just a big fish in a small pond. I perceived this response as her telling me that she didn't think I could do it. I was hurt by her lack of confidence and felt unsupported. To my credit, I did not change my goals. As a matter of fact, I saw it as a greater challenge now. I wanted to prove to her that I could do it.

I made varsity, started some games, and earned a letter. With some athletic success under my belt, my confidence began to increase. I decided to give football another shot the next year.

The summer before my junior season I had grown to be 6 feet, 5 inches tall and 270 pounds. I was already receiving letters from colleges showing some interest in offering me some sort of scholarship. I began to realize that football might be the only avenue for me to pursue my dream of a life in professional athletics. I committed myself to work hard that year. I was going to learn the game and become a dominating player.

What a disappointment my junior year became. It seemed like the harder I tried, the harder it became to improve. My focus went from a having a pro career to earning a college scholarship to just working on getting good right where I was. I played better that year but not nearly to my potential.

It had gotten back to me that some of the seniors and a few guys from my own class were saying that the reason I wasn't very good was because I just wasn't tough enough. I couldn't play with the big boys, and I had come from that wimpy little Christian school. This made me angry. But, even worse, I became extremely discouraged.

Basketball season saved me once again, as I started every game and played well. I was selected as the most improved player on the team. I credit my continued improvement to the imaginary battles with the basketball greats I was still having in my backyard and the fact that I truly enjoyed the game itself.

The next summer right before the start of football, I began to think of how much I disliked the hard work of trying to get better for a sport I had yet to learn to enjoy. I had run and lifted all summer with the goal of just being good in high school, and had really focused on doing the little things it took to get better, just as I had earlier with basketball. But the improvement was coming so slowly that it was hard for me to see any at all. I was not looking forward to another season of disappointment.

Feeling discouraged, I started to weaken in my commitment to my childhood dream of being a pro athlete. I actually got to the point where two days before practices were to start I told two of my teammates that I was thinking of quitting. Right away they told me I shouldn't quit. They said they needed me to win the state championship, and that had been their goal since junior high. I told them I would think about it but to please not tell anyone. The next day at workouts a coach came up to me and told me he had heard I was considering quitting. I shot a look at my two teammates and thought, *How could they have violated my trust*? I turned to the coach and admitted my discouragement and that the rumor had some truth to it. He went on to tell me that he had never seen a kid come through that school with as much potential who was willing to work as hard as I did. He assured me that if I continued to play the game and work hard, it was only a matter of time before it would come together for me. I thanked him and then asked him to please not tell my dad.

My father, who was 6 feet, 6 inches tall and weighed 300 pounds, met me at the door that evening as I returned home from practice. The first words out of his mouth alerted me to the fact that the coach had informed him about my desire to quit the football team. We had one of those long father/son conversations where the father talks and the son agrees. He told me that he had not worked so hard and taught me so much just so that I would become someone who quits when discouraged. Deep inside, I knew what the right decision was. I really did dream of being a pro football player. And when I saw how many people believed in me, I figured I would give it my best shot for one more year. I decided that I was going to follow through with my commitment.

My habit was to work hard. Even though I wasn't excited about being at practice, I was going to try while I was there. Then, all of a sudden, it happened. It all fell together and I'll never forget it. Two weeks into practices, I was faced off, one on one, with one of the guys who had made fun of me in junior high. I heard the word "hike," and when I hit him I stepped, dipped my hips, ripped up with my fists against his chest and lifted him right off the ground. I knew this because I took the time to look down, and I could see his feet dangling below us. Taking him back a few yards and slamming him to the ground, I landed on top of him and he made that sound that I grew to love. It is difficult to capture in writing, but here it goes. He said, "AARRRUUURRGGHHH!" Or something like that. I jumped up feeling no pain myself, but I knew I had inflicted some on him and told the quarterback to run that play again. Again the same result. I had it! I had learned the technique. The rest of the story is truly like a fairy tale. I continued to work hard that season and concentrate on being the best tackle at Snohomish High School. The rest took care of itself.

We ended the season undefeated and won the State Championship. And I began to love the game of football. Colleges called from all over the country. I was voted All-this team and All-that team and even selected as the nation's Lineman of the Year by a couple of magazines. Every award was a shock to me. All I was really focused on that entire year was to be good right where I was. I wanted to prove my critics wrong, and I did. Even now I continue to win awards for my performance that year in football. (Recently, I was named the starting right tackle on the state of Washington's

All-Century high school football team.) A very successful college and pro career was soon to follow.

I wouldn't mind taking all the credit for my meteoric rise to stardom in football, but I can't. The real credit goes to people around me—people who believed in me. Those who saw in me what I couldn't see in myself and took the step to challenge me are responsible for me making the right decision in the face of adversity and doubt. I was busy trying to build a wall to keep out the pain of failure when my teammates, my coach, and my dad would not let me do it. They encouraged me to get past that wall, and I did. What if I had confided in another discouraged player, and we talked each other into quitting together? Where would I be now if my father had not challenged me to follow through? I don't even want to think of the consequences those actions would have had on my life.

Even now, I need the same type of supportive people around me. Working toward my dream of influencing people with my message of hope, I have encountered numerous tough times. School administrators have been skeptical to bring me to their school because they stereotyped me as a jock. Some schools have resisted because they feel that motivational assemblies aren't as important as students spending time in the classroom, working on academics. Or they are discouraged because their last speaker did not hit the mark. And businesses have been reluctant at times because of my lack of business experience, regardless of the strength of my message and the empowerment it could bring to their employees. All of these circumstances can be frustrating.

In addition to the fickle market, there was the reality that my income was not as steady as it was when I worked for the City of Everett. The financial risk of leaving my job, which was worth about $100,000 a year including benefits, was not a small one. In those times of uncertainty and self-doubt, I would question whether I should continue. I needed the support of encouraging teammates.

Thankfully, I am blessed with the best. My wife Pam and I started dating in high school, and she has been my partner in life ever since. She lived through the ups and downs right by my side. She has always supported my endeavors. Her belief in my passions and dreams is sometimes the only thing that gets me over the tough times. She reminds me of how far we've come and how important it is to dream and follow our dreams. She instills in me the confidence I lack in those times of weakness. She sacrificed when we needed to because she shared my dream.

Not unlike their mother, our children are wonderful, too. They are dreamers and doers themselves and are very supportive of dad's pursuits. They continue to remind me that the relationships I develop and the people I love and am loved by are the only meaningful measures of the wealth I can attain in this life. I especially like when they see me getting discouraged or stressed out and one of them tells me to practice what I preach. I could not have a better core of support.

It takes all of your personal ingredients plus some help to succeed. You need your dream, a plan, courageous decisions, and your support system to help you find the ability to be consistent when you are weak. At all times, surround yourself with people you know will be encouragers in your life . . . not discouragers. But more importantly, make a commitment to be an encourager to those who need your support.

9

BE GREAT RIGHT WHERE YOU ARE

"Some people are great dreamers, planners, and talkers, but never take the time to shut up and work on simply getting better today."

I am always surprised when a mother approaches me with little Tommy in tow and proceeds to tell me how he is going to be a pro football player. My first concern is Tommy. Is this his dream or his parents'? Then she asks a question concerning the secret to making it big in sports. I am asked to give some quick and dirty insider advice on how Tommy can jump on the fast track to athletic stardom. I think most people are disappointed with my answer. I tell them that there is no secret. If becoming a pro football player is truly what Tommy wants to do with his life, then his number one concern should be devising a plan to get better today than he was yesterday. And then better the next day than he was the day before. There is no fast track or secret to success in anything. Success comes from putting together all of the things we have already talked about: a positive attitude, dreams, goals, plans, good decisions, decisive action, a strong support system, and good old-fashioned hard work. To be great in the future you must first work to be great right where you are. The rest will take care of itself.

I was not the best athlete on my high school football team. However, I did get the most scholarship offers. I was not the best athlete on my college football team. Yet I was the only one drafted in the first round by the NFL. I was not the most athletic offensive lineman that the Raiders had drafted over the previous two decades. Nevertheless, I was the first rookie to start on the Raider offensive line since Gene Upshaw had 16 years earlier. The key for me in every case is that I took pride in believing that I worked harder than anyone else on my team.

I can remember going into the Raiders summer training camp in such great shape that during camp I actually lost some of my conditioning. I had worked so hard during the off-season that getting into shape was not a concern. The two practices a day at camp were nowhere near as challenging as the ones Keith Gilbertson Sr. had put me through during the off-season. Coach, as I called him, was one of my high school coaches and is a genuine hero and role model. For many years, he had coached several sports, including track and field. He had even coached a couple of Olympic athletes. Coach had the credentials to get me into shape and volunteered to work me to death twice a day, every day of the off-season. We worked together from before my freshman year at the University of Washington until I retired from football.

Through the years, Coach invested his own time and energy and would not allow me to pay him a dime. Sometimes I wondered if he was just the sort of sick person who loves to watch people suffer. But I knew that was not true. He shared my dream and wanted to see me succeed as badly as I did. I love him for his support and help in teaching me more about what hard work can accomplish. I owe a great deal of the success I have experienced to Coach's support.

Being in such great shape going into training camp was like picking the best branches before the great tree races I described earlier. It gave me an advantage to succeed in a very competitive environment. While the other linemen in camp were trying to get into shape, I could be working on the advanced parts of my game. It was like having a 10-meter head start in a 100-meter race.

I did not provide the previous list of my football accomplishments to brag or make the point of how great I was. Quite the contrary. I am sharing these examples because they illustrate that hard work can tip the scales in your favor when you are not as gifted as your competition. In addition, hard work and self-discipline are the only answers for competing against yourself to be better tomorrow than you are today. This is a lesson that was taught early to me by my father.

My father had a scholarship to play both football and basketball at a college in the northwest. But during his second year, with a wife and child to support and me on the way, he had to quit and find work. An intelligent man who learned his work ethic from his father, my dad did several types of labor and even some engineering design work. Years later, when I was still young, the company he worked for went on strike. My father was out of work for months and the bills were piling up. He looked for work diligently, but the surrounding area had very few opportunities for employment. Then one day my mother sent him out the door with a sack lunch and told him not to come home until he had found a job. How's that for pressure? He didn't have to worry though, as he came home that night announcing he had landed a job driving a forklift for a company on the Seattle waterfront.

Seattle was at least an hour commute for my father, which may not seem like that much now but was quite a distance to drive to work in those days. While he worked there, he began doing what he had done at all of his previous jobs: he showed up a little early and stayed a little late. Then he started doing things to make his job more fun. He did this by competing against himself. Each day he would try to beat his previous records for the number of forklift runs or the amount of product he had stacked. Sometimes he would finish his assigned work before the others and make a game of trying to figure out what needed to be done next and finish it before he was asked to do it. He found great pleasure in receiving a new assignment and being able to tell the supervisor he had already finished it.

Dad started getting a reputation for being a hard worker, but his efforts were not always popular with his fellow workers because it forced them to try and keep up. On the other hand, his reputation enticed his managers to watch more closely. When the warehouse supervisor job became available, my father got it. He proceeded to perform that job in the same fashion as the last, and when the next management position opened up, he was promoted again.

My father worked for that company for nearly thirty years, the last fifteen or so as the Senior Vice President of Marine Operations. I am proud of what he was able to accomplish because of his hard work and ingenuity. Sometimes, hard work will make up for a lack of focus or abilities in other areas needed for success. When you combine the dream, the plan, the decisions, the actions, the courage to be consistent, and the ingredient of hard work, you are nearly unstoppable.

My dad was not perfect. Just like me, he made mistakes. But the positive impact he had on me far outweighs any of the negative ones. I could not have achieved nearly what I have without the lessons he taught me. I remember my first job. My older brother Daron was twelve, and my dad said it was time for him to get a summer job. This was the early '70s, obviously before the current child labor laws. We lived in Snohomish, Washington, which was and still is primarily a farming area. The work for kids my brother's age was on the farms doing what we called haying. The farmers would cut the grass on their open fields and, after letting it dry for a few days, would use a machine to turn the grass into bales of hay.

These bales would lie in the fields until crews could drive through and stack them on a truck to be taken to the barn. Once they got to the barn, the bales of hay would be unloaded and restacked. It was hard, dirty work. The average bale weighed nearly 60 pounds when it was dry and even more if it got wet from the rain.

I happened to walk through the room as my father was talking on the phone to a farmer, setting my brother Daron up with his first haying job. He looked up at me and said to the guy, "Yes, I have two boys that would like to work tomorrow." I was wondering which of Daron's poor friends my dad had committed to the job, when he hung up the phone and told me where I was going to be working the next day. I was just 10 years old but already bigger than my older brother, and my dad thought it would be a good experience for me.

Most of the kids working the farms were older teenagers, and I was scared to death that I wouldn't fit in with them. I was also afraid of failing. I didn't know what they were going to have me do or even if I would be able to do it, and I tried to convince my dad that I was too young and scared. I told him I didn't think I could do it and didn't want to. He then sat me down on his lap and told me I didn't have anything to worry about. He explained that if I just did three things while I was there, the farmer would be happy with my effort and treat me well.

"First," he said, "whatever he asks you to do, do it and then do a little bit more. Second, never make him have to tell you to do the same thing twice. And third, no matter what work he asks you to do, give it your best effort. There may be some things you can't do. You are only ten and not as fully developed as some of the other guys there. But never fail at an assignment because you weren't willing to try."

I went on to have many profitable summers in the Snohomish

Valley, and have never forgotten the advice my dad gave me that day. I have used it many times in nearly every endeavor of my life. Imagine how productive any team or work group could be if they applied these same three principles.

Throughout the years, I have consistently applied these principles in every career endeavor. I have found that when I am focusing on the little things, when I am concentrating on just achieving the goal of getting better each and every day, that is when I have reached the big goals. Some people are great dreamers, planners, and talkers, but never take the time to shut up and work on simply getting better today. Most of the awards I have won in athletics and youth work have come as a surprise to me. They have been almost an afterthought of just getting the work done.

I am committed to improving my ability to communicate my message every time I have an opportunity to enter a school or business. I am working so hard today to encourage and motivate those listening that I know the commitment and hard work will be rewarded with continued success in the future. Your key to becoming great in the future is to concentrate on being great right where you are and being better today than you were yesterday.

I feel fortunate to have had many varied experiences from which to learn. Much of what I have learned has come from those experiences, but a great deal was taught by special people such as my father and Coach. These individuals have shown me much more than just what it takes for me to succeed. By their actions they have handed down a legacy illustrating what it takes to lead others successfully.

10

LEADERSHIP AND SUCCESS

"Earning the respect of others does not come by setting high standards or even enforcing them. It comes by living by those standards yourself."

With success comes the responsibility to lead. Those who live life successfully will encounter situations where leadership skills are required. Like it or not, people look to those who have achieved as role models worthy of being emulated. I believe it is the responsibility of the person being emulated to behave in such a way as to provide honorable leadership to those who are following. Leadership, both good and bad, is learned throughout our lives.

As I reflect on the skills, principles and philosophies that have led to the successes in my life, it's obvious that people and circumstances have influenced me and my beliefs. For some of us, the most valuable insights we possess are learned from the most unlikely people and/or circumstances. By avoiding a difficult situation or person, you may be passing up the only opportunity to learn something you would not learn anywhere else. Every person we meet and every circumstance we encounter can teach us something if we are open to learning and being taught. Sports taught me so much more about life than I ever expected. And much of what I believe about leadership was learned through my athletic experiences.

As a football player for many years, I had developed my own opinions about what made a good coach and what made a bad one. I had played for some assistant coaches who fell into the bad coach category. There were times when I was certain that I knew more than they did. I believed that, if given the chance, I could do a much better job. My mom used to tell me to be careful what I wished for because I just might get it. I now understand her warnings.

After retiring from the NFL, I was approached by the owner of a northwest area semi-pro football franchise. They were involved in the establishment of a new league that was called the Minor League Football System. The league consisted of twelve teams from twelve different cities in the United States. The players would not be paid, but all of their equipment and travel expenses would be taken care of during the twelve game season. The teams would also help find the players local jobs to support themselves and their families. The league was supposed to attract the best of the semi-pro players and others fresh out of college who were still looking for a chance to play in the NFL.

When initially approached, I was intrigued by the idea of coaching and applying the ideas I had learned while playing. Certainly I could be better than some of the coaches I had. But I knew it would take a great deal of time, and I did have my vending business to run. So I decided I would agree to coach the team, but would ask for a much higher salary than I thought the owner would be willing to pay. Much to my surprise, he agreed to my terms. I was the new head coach of the Seattle Express football team of the MLFS. It was time to walk around in that greener grass on the other side of the fence for a while.

As a coach, I discovered very quickly that the grass wasn't any greener and, as a matter of fact, it wasn't even edible. My biggest hurdle was trying to convince players that they didn't already know more than the coaches did. Imagine that! At first it was very hard for me to cut anyone who tried out. They were all trying so hard and they weren't even going to get paid. I kept players on the team who had some attitude problems, but I figured I could earn their trust and respect over time, and they would settle down.

Being head coach meant dealing with guys that I knew would eventually drive me nuts. These included the biggest, strongest athlete on my team, who couldn't remember a play or his assignments for five minutes. Talk about frustrating! I began to think it was my coaching, but later learned that he had always battled a poor memory.

I remember a particular two-hour flight to California. I was sitting behind a couple of players, one of whom was also having a difficult time retaining information. Just after takeoff the captain came on the loudspeaker and announced that we had hit a flock of birds and they had gone through one of the three engines on the plane and disabled it. The captain assured us that there was no danger because the plane was designed to fly on two engines without any problems. The only issue was that there was going to be an additional thirty minutes added to our flight time. About one hour later we heard a loud thump on the right side of the airplane. The captain immediately came on the loudspeaker to tell us we had just lost another engine. Again he assured us that there was no real danger, and that this airplane was perfectly capable of reaching our destination on the one engine remaining. However, we were going to be an additional thirty minutes late. Right after this announcement the "genius" in front of me turned to the player next to him and said, "Jeez, I sure hope we don't lose that last engine or it will take us forever to get there." I thought it was a joke before I realized he was serious. If that wasn't bad enough, the guy next to him shook his head and said, "Yeah." These were the types of people with whom I was trying to win football games.

The worst were those with attitude problems. Midway through the season I realized that my idea of being light handed from the start was not working out too well. Our record was three and three: three losses at home and three losses away. I obviously was not in control of my team. Players were taking advantage of my leniency, and I needed to tighten my grip. I started by cutting the worst attitude offender on the team. The only mistake I made was cutting him on the plane in the middle of a four-hour flight. The rest of the flight was spent listening to his apologies and promises to be better, as well as the heartfelt lobbying by the one player that was his friend. It was an agonizing two hours. The rest of the season was consumed with wrestling control of my team back from the players to whom I had unwittingly given it, through my lack of clear standards and strict discipline.

The most powerful lesson I learned from this experience was that when I am put into a leadership role, I must immediately establish a set of standards that will provide a strong foundation to build from. These standards must be set high and expectations must be made perfectly clear. By establishing high standards and clear expectations and then enforcing them fairly and consistently, you can loosen your grip to reward good behavior. It is nearly impossible to tighten the grip on something over which you never had control.

One of my biggest breakthroughs was when I realized that it was much more important to be respected than liked when functioning in a leadership role. Earning the respect of others does not come by setting high standards or even enforcing them. It comes by living by those standards yourself. No two leaders epitomized this statement better than my high school and college head football coaches.

Coach Dick Armstrong retired from Snohomish High School with the most wins as a high school football coach in Washington state history. The greatest compliment I can give Dick Armstrong as a coach is that in all of the football I learned following my high school experience, I was never taught any of the fundamental aspects of the game any differently than he had taught them. The greatest gift he gave me as a person was taking "Curt Marsh the boy" and helping me to become "Curt Marsh the man."

He consistently expected nothing less than my best effort, which he always felt was more than I was giving him at the time. Even during my senior year, when I was playing much better than I understood and our team was undefeated, he would focus on the three best players—Jerry Mclain, Chris Utt, and myself—and accuse us of not trying hard enough. He would single us out to run plays in practice because of his professed disappointment in our mediocre efforts. No matter how hard we worked, we never could work hard enough to please him. He was the type of coach you disliked while you played for him because he was constantly pushing you to improve—good was never good enough. However, when I finished playing for him and looked back on the experience, I could not help but feel an overwhelming gratitude for what he taught me as a person. He instilled a confidence in me that I could overcome any obstacle if I worked hard enough. He taught me to never be satisfied with an effort that was just "good enough." Even though I didn't like him much when he coached me, I always feared and respected him. As I got older we became good friends. I didn't fear him anymore, but I still respected him.

Coach Armstrong has since passed away and we don't see him in person anymore. However, we can still see his legacy through the passing of the valuable gifts he gave to everyone who had the chance to play for him. Our friends and relatives benefit. Our children benefit as we pass on the lessons he taught. And they will, in turn, pass them on to their children.

Another example of a great and respected leader is Coach Don

James, the most organized and consistent man I have ever met. When Coach James tells you something, you might as well carve it in stone because it will not change until he says so. If you are not able to live up to the expectations that have been made clear to you, you will pay the price until you can. Coach James ran the University of Washington football program like a great CEO runs a successful corporation. He made the rules and called the shots, but he empowered his assistants to carry the message to the players.

Coach James hired bright and talented assistant coaches, many of whom went on to become head and assistant coaches in the NFL. Under his leadership, he gave the assistants full authority and responsibility to interact with their assigned position players in meetings and on the field. During practices, Coach James stayed in a tower that was about twenty feet high and positioned in the middle of the sideline so he could view the entire field. He took notes and seldom said a word. Just his presence was intimidating enough to make you feel that he was watching you personally at all times. If a player warranted a comment from Coach James from the tower, you knew he had really done something terrible. He never yelled at or even corrected an assistant coach during practice or any other time in front of players. Later I heard stories of how Coach James would reprimand or correct them behind closed doors, but the players were always taught to respect and listen to their direct authority, the assistant coach. This was Coach James' way of maintaining clear, well-defined lines of authority that no player could question.

As a player, I began to feel as though Coach James was aloof and not interested in the personal lives of his players. He always said he had an open door policy, but no one had the guts to walk through the door. I found it hard to understand how a man who seemed so genuinely caring during the recruiting phase of the relationship could be so distant and uninterested in really getting to know his players, as his assistants did. Coach James was never abusive or berating, he was just extremely serious and focused on the task at hand. If someone had asked me if I liked Coach James while I was playing for him, I would have told them I didn't know him well enough to say, but that I sure respected his authority.

The fact that Coach James did not engage me or any other players in playful conversation bothered me until I finished playing for him. But after my senior season was over and Coach James no longer had the responsibility as my head coach, he seemed to change and became that genuinely nice, caring individual I had met while he was recruiting me. It was not until then that I began to understand that the relationship he had with me as a player under his leadership was completely different than the one he could have with me as a former player and peer. Today, Don James is one of the most caring men I know. He and his wife, Carol, were among the first people to visit me after my amputation. Carol brought homemade cookies, and we visited for quite a while. Coach James is very responsive to requests made to him by former players, such as playing in golf tournaments or speaking for special occasions. And he treats those who played for him as though they were a part of some special second family.

I came to understand the wisdom and intelligence of this great college coach and College Football Hall of Fame member. Coach James had a responsibility to lead his players and coaches toward a common goal. In that role he was our leader, not our buddy. He was a master at planning and organization, but I believe his greatest leadership trait was his consistency. When Coach James spoke, everyone listened. We became players and coaches committed to maintaining our own consistency of self-discipline and attaining goals, simply because of the expectations and example of our leader. I believe Don James ranks as one of the greatest college football coaches of all time for three reasons: commitment, consistency and integrity. He not only required these traits from his teams, he lived them in his own life.

Like Don James, good leaders must have integrity. Integrity starts with honesty, which is difficult to maintain consistently in a world so accepting of little white lies. Recently, I read a newspaper article about a survey conducted among top Fortune 500 companies. In the survey, employees were asked *What do you want most from a supervisor*? The number one answer was honesty. Becoming a great leader requires that you do the hard work up front, and that hard work includes being honest at all times. In other words, it is much more important to share the truth with those looking to you for leadership than to lie, postpone, or hide the truth.

I have not always followed my own advice of being honest with those I was attempting to lead. As a result, I have felt the pain of being trapped in the web of deceit that one small lie can create, and I have seen the mistrust that is created when bosses mislead their employees. Even if the motive for deception seems honorable, such as lessening pain for the person you are misleading, a good leader will do the hard work up front by being frank and honest. Often times, those in leadership roles are asked to be the bearer of bad news to those they supervise or represent. The temptation is to sugar-coat the information or even distort the truth in such a way as to not inflict too much pain upon delivery, or create conflict between you and the one you lead. In these situations, honesty is always your best bet. However, being honest does not preclude the need to deliver the message with compassion and respect. Learning to be completely honest with those that you are leading will help assure a consistent, respectful relationship.

Even when it has been difficult, being an honest leader has helped me a great deal. As the recreation superintendent for the City of Everett, I took pride in the fact that I was open and honest with my employees. This honesty, I believe, is what earned their trust and respect. As a result, we were able to work together to accomplish a great deal in a short amount of time. I am satisfied when someone

I am leading can say *I don't necessarily agree with everything Curt says, but at least I always know were he stands on an issue or decision.* It is exhausting and frustrating when a follower has to constantly guess what the ulterior motives of their leader might be. (This is also true in the world of parenting.) The more the guessing game continues, the less trust and respect there will be.

If you are able to do the hard work up front and lead with honesty and integrity, you will avoid the huge messes down the road. But you must be willing to endure the immediate pain that telling the truth may cause, or you will most certainly create more pain and distrust later and compromise your ability to lead effectively.

I believe that a key to my effectiveness as a motivator of youth and even my own kids is trustworthiness. Young people can pick out a phony a mile away. If you are going to walk into a school gymnasium with poor acoustics and 1,500 kids who may not want to be there, and talk to them for an hour, you had better be sincere. You had better be honest and have the integrity to tell them the truth about yourself and life. Teenagers are looking for leadership from adults who they can believe truly care about them. They are skeptical of adults and society, in general. Whether dealing with gang-involved kids or the school's valedictorian, we must communicate in truth. We must respect the youth's circumstances and emotional pain without compromising our own beliefs and integrity. And we must be real with them or they will not allow us the opportunity to lead. Interestingly, adults are also looking for this same honesty and integrity from those in positions of leadership.

Sadly, all leaders suffer—even the honest ones—when some have been found to be untruthful. For instance, the prospect for all elected officials to lead effectively is undermined by the cynicism and mistrust created by the former indiscretions of others. Instead of breeding confidence and teamwork, these leaders are forced to wade through skepticism and division. We will never be successful unless those who are looking to us for leadership are able to commit to our common goals with the confidence that we are trustworthy.

As my venture grows and as my family grows, more and more people will become a part of the big picture. Understanding my responsibility to lead in a way that is honorable and effective is extremely important to the success of both.

Becoming a leader is in the natural progression of one who lives life successfully. Continuing to live successfully demands that one must continue to learn. No person is too smart or too old to learn. I am still looking for new and innovative tools to help me lead others and myself to live life in the most successful way possible. Life can be a continuous learning process if you are open to the discoveries. The same quest for constant improvement that enables you to reach one dream is necessary to move you on to the next one. Being better tomorrow than you are today is a job that is never finished.

11

EMBRACING DIVERSITY AND ITS TRUE COLORS

"The most effective leaders are those who recognize the strength of diversity."

Great leadership comes from the knowledge that you are only as successful as the people you lead. I have a framed plaque on my wall to remind me of a truth about great leadership. It reads, "A good leader inspires others with confidence in himself. A great leader inspires others with confidence in themselves." When a group accomplishes a task and can say, *We did it*! the leadership has done its job well. If there is a willingness and commitment to foster an environment of individual respect and tolerance, the entire group is empowered to work as a team and achieve great things.

The most effective leaders are those who recognize the strength of diversity. Potentially, diversity could lead to a very frustrated group that finds it difficult to work together because of the many different points of view. However, there can be awesome power in bringing together diverse talents, skills, and personalities to accomplish a common goal. If leaders are successful in helping the individuals in a group recognize and appreciate each other's differences as strengths, and can turn the group's focus toward the overall goal, the power of each individual is multiplied. The tasks required to accomplish the group's overall goal can be done according to the natural strengths of each individual team member. Thus, the entire team becomes stronger. And each individual is more fulfilled as he recognizes and takes pride in his or her unique and important contributions to the team's success.

Life is a constant learning process. There is a saying in business that goes *If you think you have got it all figured out, you obviously have no idea what is going on.* Because of the ebb and flow of constant change, I am always looking for new approaches and tools to add to my tool chest as I work on building my dreams. Recently, I discovered True Colors™, a tool that has been extremely helpful in my life. The True Colors™ concept is based on very old principles presented in a new and exciting way, and teaches us how to better understand the differences and similarities in all of us. The better we understand ourselves and others, the more likely it is that we will be successful in achieving our dreams while developing respectful, tolerant, and lasting relationships along the way.

True Colors™ is a concept that was developed by Don Lowry to translate complicated learning theory into practical information we can all understand. For centuries man has been studying fellow man. Some of the psychological studies have focused on the unique characteristics of individuals and those that are common among groups. Twenty-four centuries ago, Hypocrites identified four different types of human beings. Carl Jung described four key differences in 1921. And for the past 35 years, Dr. David Kearsey has been refining the work of Katherine C. Briggs and Isabel Briggs-Myers who developed the Myers-Briggs Type Indicator (MBTI). Through the MBTI, which is a written test, its authors show that human behavior is orderly and can be characterized by different personality types. Dr. Kearsey describes these different personality types in four groups. His work provides the basis for True Colors™.

The four personality types are denoted by the colors Blue, Gold, Green, and Orange. The theory behind True Colors™ maintains that we are all born with a Primary Color that relates to our primary personality traits. Although each of us is most influenced by our Primary Color, our personalities include aspects of the entire color spectrum in varying degrees. Our secondary color is the second most influential trait in our personality. There are even times and/or situations in which our weakest colors or traits will come to the forefront when needed. Each personality type or color has strengths, core needs, and core values that have been defined through centuries of research.

There are several benefits from using the True Colors™ system. It provides you with an opportunity to develop your understanding of your own potential, and helps you recognize and encourage the potential in others. It also teaches you to bridge the gap of communication, leading to respect and compassion for others, as well as open doors for successful relationships. In addition, True Colors™ helps you see and use different ways of supporting and rewarding other people's behaviors and values, thus strengthening the work of groups or teams.

If you are starting to dream about your future, it is extremely valuable to know that people are intrinsically different and achieve a sense of self-worth in different ways. Understanding those ways through the True Colors™ system, will help you in choosing, planning, and defining the action steps to achieve your dream or support someone else's.

The four True Colors™ and the personality traits they represent are as follows:

BLUE represents calm. People with Blue as their Primary Color value balance, harmony and relationships to people. They prefer lives free from tension. They are compassionate, encouraging, and supporting. Blues like to do things that require caring, counseling, nurturing, and harmonizing. They have a strong desire to contribute and help others lead more significant lives. They are poetic and often enjoy the arts. They value unity and integrity in relationships. Blues are enthusiastic, idealistic, communicative, and sympathetic, and express their feelings easily.

GOLD represents a need to be solid and responsible. They are driven to fulfill duties and obligations. They organize and structure their lives and the lives of others. Golds like to do things that require management and detail. They are stable, efficient, and dependable. Golds value home, family, status, security, tradition, and being practical and sensible. They are caring, concerned, and loyal. They show concern through the practical things they do.

GREEN represents persistence, determination, firmness, and consistency. Those with Green as a Primary Color value intellect and capability above all else. They depend upon information and data rather than feelings. Greens are independent thinkers, natural non-conformists, and live by their own standards. They are conceptual and have an investigative mind. They like to do things that require vision, problem solving, strategy, ingenuity, design, and change. They value knowledge, intelligence, insight, and justice. Greens enjoy relationships with shared interests. They prefer to let their heads rule their hearts. Greens are cool, calm, collected, and do not express emotions easily.

ORANGE represents energy, power and strength. Those with Orange as a Primary Color feel the will to achieve results, to win, and be successful. Orange is action: sports, struggles, eroticism, and productivity. They are courageous and act on a moment's notice. They need stimulation, freedom, and excitement. Oranges are natural leaders, troubleshooters, and performers. They are competitive and bounce back quickly from defeat. They like to do things that require variety, results, and participation. Oranges value action, resourcefulness, and courage. They are generous, charming, and impulsive, and show affection through physical contact.

Having read the previous paragraphs describing the personality traits representative of each of the colors, you can begin to identify your own Primary Color and color spectrum. As you learn more about each color's strengths and needs, the information can be used in a practical way in planning your goals, developing teams, and building relationships.

As I worked through the process of discovering my own Primary Color and color spectrum, it helped me more fully understand the whys of what I do, as well as the motivations and needs of others. I learned to appreciate the strengths I naturally possess and recognize the weaker traits in my personality. As I work to better my life day to day in pursuit of a goal or a dream, I can take advantage of the strengths I have and work to enhance the areas of weakness. What has been even more exciting is that I have learned to seek out and build alliances with individuals who are strongest in the areas of my weakness. By surrounding myself with a support system that can do the tasks I prefer not to do, or don't do well, my effectiveness in accomplishing a goal is multiplied.

I am a Primary Orange with a very strong Green second. The third color in my spectrum is Blue and lastly I have a tiny bit of Gold. To succeed in football I was able to use the Orange traits to compete and perform. My Green helped me to learn quickly and gave me the desire to master the game. My Blue gave me enough compassion to be gracious with the many people a professional athlete or anyone in the spotlight has to deal with. My Blue Color was also the reason I could come home after a day of aggressive combat on the football field and still gently embrace my wife and children. The missing ingredient was Gold. I was certainly willing to work hard and do the things necessary to become great, but I was not naturally equipped to develop and document the complex off-season workouts required to improve my athletic skills and gain the advantage over my competitors.

The most effective physical training programs are those that are meticulously planned and include goals and milestones which must be documented and linked to your progress toward your overall dream. The purpose of the training is to promote healthy, gradual improvement to insure you begin camp at the same time you reach your peak in physical conditioning. To develop such a plan would take an extremely organized mind. The successful implementation of such a plan would require detailed documentation and the self-discipline or sense of duty to do it consistently.

Looking back, armed with the information I have learned from the True Colors™ system, I was extremely fortunate that Coach Gilbertson became my partner for all of those years. Coach is a primary Gold and thoroughly enjoyed doing all of the detailed preparation and documentation. Even when I did not feel like working out, I knew I had to go because Coach was going to be there, come Hell or high water. After making the commitment to work with me, he saw it as his duty to be there each and every day, right on time and ready to work. He expected the same from me.

Combining my weaknesses with Coach's strengths was the key to my off-season success that led to success on the field. I got lucky and fell into that relationship, not recognizing the potential of our two personality types supporting one another. But I know now that in order for me to be successful, I must align myself with people who possess the strengths of Gold.

These same principles come into play when you are working with teams. The most successful teams could be the ones with each of the Primary Colors represented in their group. If the group can recognize and learn to appreciate the differences in their personality traits, the tasks of the group to reach their overall goal could be divided and done according to the natural strengths and needs of each individual.

When I consider the different individuals on our 1983 Super Bowl Championship Team and realize how many different Primary Colors we had working together as one cohesive unit, it is no wonder we were powerful.

Coach Tom Flores was extremely organized and most probably a Gold. Practices were meticulously planned, and detailed game plans were developed. He was also known as a player's coach, which means the players knew he was genuinely concerned with their well-being. This was probably due to a strong Blue influence in his personality. These traits were valuable assets to our team, but one of his weaknesses was in the area of motivating people. So, recognizing that others on the team could effectively play that role, he let them do it.

We had a group of veteran players who were strong motivators and instilled an attitude in each player to fear nothing and no one. People like Ted Hendricks, John Matuszack, Rod Martin, Lester Hayes, Mike Davis, and Lyle Alzado led verbally and through their style of play, and they were vital to our success. The Primary Color of these action-oriented individuals was probably Orange.

I had teammates who demanded perfection from themselves and others. Failure was not an option for guys like Howie Long, Matt Millen, Bill Pickel, Charley Hannah and Marcus Allen. Despite their God-given talents, they were committed to working at mastering their positions and responsibilities. This led others with less talent to do the same, and made our entire team stronger. I would bet that all of these players were Primary Green individuals. These people led by example.

We also had those who were the glue that held us together by their efforts to create an environment of unity and camaraderie. This was a group of Blues. Led by Dave Dalby, other players like Steve Sylvester, Bob Nelson, and Jim Plunkett put together special events, such as an air hockey tournament and a "rookie party," to promote togetherness and get us through the intensity of training camp. During the season they organized an event after every Thursday practice called "Camaraderie." Everyone was invited to an eating establishment in town that cleared a large area for the team. We ate and drank together with the sole purpose of enjoying each other's company, laughing and enhancing friendships. These guys led by keeping the team together.

For that one season, that group of guys with diverse personalities and skills pulled together as one. We were the best in the world. Everyone had his role and played it well. We found ways to accept and appreciate the many differences among us and focused on one goal—winning the Super Bowl.

I wish I had learned the True Colors™ system earlier for the benefit of my family. Communicating with teenagers is almost always difficult. But it can be nearly impossible when they are your own children. In fairness, it is probably just as hard for them to understand where adults are coming from. With the insight of the color spectrums of my wife and children, I feel much more confident that I can position myself to understand their points of view.

My whole family has done their color spectrums, and it is interesting how much diversity there can be within one home. My wife is Gold with a Green secondary color, thank God. Jake, the artist, is as Blue as they come with some Green spattered in. CJ, the athlete, is an Orange with Green a close second. Jillian is Orange with a strong Blue secondary influence.

With the knowledge of my family members' natural strengths, weaknesses, needs, and values, it becomes easier to appreciate their points of view. And with a better understanding of what motivates our children, Pam and I have been more effective in communicating our desires as parents in ways that our children can identify with and more easily connect to. It can work the same way in reverse when a child or teen is trying to communicate with an adult. If they know what the adult's Primary Color is, they, too, can learn to communicate in a language that mom and dad will understand.

Our personalities are a large part of who we are. By understanding both the similarities and differences that our personalities create, we are able to tolerate, respect, and more fully cooperate with others.

One detail I did not mention is that my wife, Pam, is of African-American descent. I did not mention it because I seldom think of it. When I look at my wife I see her for who she is. We are not black and white. We are Pam and Curt. I recognize her inner being—her personality—and she sees me the same way. By perceiving each other according to *who* we are, our attention is focused there and not on the color of our skin. Regardless of race, religion, or economic status, our personalities are what make us tick from the inside out.

I have spent a good deal of time explaining the True Colors™ system and have just scratched the surface, considering the potential uses of this effective tool. The reason for including it in this book is threefold. First, I believe that seeking to understand yourself and others better should be a goal for everyone. Relationships are the true wealth to be acquired while on this earth. Secondly, I want to emphasize that at 40 years of age, I am still searching for new and innovative tools to help me live my life in the most successful way possible. And third, this tool is the best I have come across for helping us deal with the issues of understanding, accepting, and embracing diversity. It is a tremendous way to teach tolerance, respect, and cooperation. And everyone can benefit from the insight True Colors™ offers.

For me to be successful in my dreams for the future, I must develop relationships that are based on mutual respect. I am committed to lead those who work with me in a way that embraces their diversity. The prospects of my success have been greatly increased with my awareness of my own color spectrum and the knowledge that it is essential to surround myself with people of diverse Primary Colors, in order for me to be at full strength.

I am always looking to improve. Climbing the mountain of self-improvement can seem like a never-ending struggle. Frustration comes when we forget that living successfully is a journey and not a destination. We can never reach the top. Many strive for success their whole lives but never feel as though they attain it. No matter how much recognition they have received or money they have earned, they have yet to feel fulfilled. Others have found a way to achieve a successful, fulfilling journey. They do this by making the well-being of the people they meet along the way the focus of their journey.

12

SUCCESS, FULFILLMENT, OR BOTH?

"Success in life is not about what you can get from the world, but rather what you can leave with it."

Living successfully is a journey. It is a lifestyle. It does not have a beginning and an end. When we think of success we often try to measure it in terms of how much money or recognition we have earned. When thinking in those terms, how much is enough? Bill Gates is worth billions of dollars and known all over the world. Does that make him a successful man? If it does, then does that mean that those who have not made as much money are not successful yet? If this were true, everyone other than Mr. Gates would be labeled a failure. If you believe money or fame defines success and leads to fulfillment, you will be disappointed. Enough is never enough.

I have had national recognition and plenty of money at times in my life. I can tell you from firsthand experience that if you define success as becoming rich and famous, and believe you will find happiness in that, you will be greatly disappointed. The whole premise is a lie. Ask anyone who has experienced it.

Don't get me wrong. I work hard to earn enough money so that my family can live comfortably, have their needs met, and have some opportunities to enjoy this beautiful world and its splendor. And I aspire to be independently wealthy so that I may someday have the freedom to spend my time and energies where I choose.

But as I stated earlier in the book, those who live the most successful working lives are those who can support themselves by doing something they enjoy and have a passion for. In my view a custodian who can support his family and likes his job is better off than a millionaire who dislikes his work.

Over the last few years, I have realized that success in life is not about what you can get from the world, but rather what you can leave with it. I was an opening speaker at a banquet in my hometown of Snohomish a couple of years ago. The keynote speaker was Phil Smart, a man I had never met but whose name I recognized. Mr. Smart is an extremely successful Seattle area businessman and is now semi-retired. He built one of the largest Mercedes Benz dealerships in the Northwest, which his son now owns and operates. Phil's presentation inspired me and helped me realize that one can achieve great financial success and find fulfillment at the same time. He had lived life successfully for years and was kind enough to share his secret.

Sixty-eight years ago, Phil joined the Cub Scouts and has been involved with Scouting ever since. When Phil reached the rank and age that ended his ability to be a Scout, his Scout leader took him aside and encouraged him to stay involved. Phil felt he had accrued a debt of sorts because of the wonderful times Scouting had given him as a boy, and it was time to start paying it back. He immediately volunteered as the Cub Master of the same group that he had joined years before. Through this experience, Phil began to learn the true meaning of success in life.

After nearly thirty years, Phil stepped down as a Scout leader. Although still involved as a supporter of Scouting, he had more time to focus on his growing business ventures. One day, while working at his desk in his car dealership, a woman who called herself Grandma Christmas stopped by to visit. She was selling Christmas cards to raise money for Children's Hospital in Seattle. Phil was so moved by their discussion that he bought the whole lot from her. Grandma Christmas could sense the helpful, caring spirit that everyone who comes in contact with Phil Smart feels and asked him what he did in his spare time. Phil told her he had just stepped down from being a Scout leader and had been focusing more on making his business a success. As she was leaving, she turned and told Phil she had an idea of how he could spend his free time and said she would be in touch with him.

A couple of days later, a member of the Board of Directors from Children's Hospital called Phil and asked if he would be willing to be their first-ever male evening volunteer. The commitment would be limited to three hours every Wednesday evening. His job would be to do whatever he could to help the staff and children. Phil told the board member that he would have to talk it over with his wife, whom he refers to as Precious. One night a week for only three hours did not seem like a huge commitment to the Smart family, especially compared to the hours Phil was used to donating to Scouts. He called the hospital and volunteered.

That was 38 years ago. In nearly four decades of volunteering at what Phil calls "The Miracle House," he has learned a great deal. Phil tells people that he goes to school every Wednesday night and that his teachers are the children. He is proud to be taking courses in strength, pain, fear, toughness, courage, heartache, forgiveness, and many other incredibly inspiring subjects. He has the greatest teachers in the world because they teach from their own experiences.

In addition to being the Wednesday evening ward volunteer, Phil has been Santa Claus every year at Children's Hospital. He spends his holidays with those little souls who are forced to celebrate while enduring the pain and seclusion of a hospital bed. Phil has watched 23 of his young friends leave this world, and he remembers each one by name and the lessons they left with him. He believes that the children, to whom he has given so much of his time and love, have given much more to him in return.

Over the past eight years, Phil has talked to over 41,000 people, sharing the stories and lessons he has learned from his years of volunteering in Scouts and at Children's Hospital. At the core of his message is the philosophy that everyone has the same 24 hours in their day. Usually eight hours are spent sleeping and eight hours are for working. It is what you choose to do with the third eight hours that defines who you are and what you have really accomplished in your life. In addition to volunteering, Phil has spent much of his third eight hours investing in his own family. He has successfully raised his children to become outstanding adults, while maintaining a strong, loving relationship with his wife.

When you ask Phil to describe success, he shares many different versions of the same theme and inspires you with quotes such as, "The true measure of your life is not the duration but the donation. How much will you be missed when you are gone?" Phil believes the most valuable asset that any of us possess is our time. What we do with that time defines how much the world will miss us. He says the only real lasting impression one can make in this life is to change the world. The best way for an individual to change the world is by helping one person at a time.

As the world generally defines success, Phil would certainly be a candidate. He has built an outstanding business and made lots of money. He is well-known and widely respected by thousands. His financial success has come with the price of hard work and dedication, combined with the passion to serve his customers in the best ways possible. All of these accomplishments were achieved by using some of the same principles described in this book. But when you talk to Phil about all of his achievements and rewards, he does not lay claim to any of them as his own. Phil believes that he, just as every one of us, has been blessed with the many gifts he has received as a result of his efforts. He is simply a steward who has been entrusted with these possessions for the purpose of using them where they are most needed.

When asked how and why he finds the time and resources to volunteer in addition to all of his other commitments, Phil says it is easy. He illustrates this by holding both hands out, palms up, and describing the gifts he has been given—praise, respect, time, recognition, money—as being put into his left hand. As his left hand begins to overflow, the result of his diligence on this earth, he has to find a place to put the gifts. He gradually transfers them into his right hand, which soon becomes full. As his left hand begins to fill up again, he must find a new place to put the gifts he holds in his right hand so he can grab the overflow of new stuff from his left. It is then that Phil finds opportunities to give some of himself away by sharing his gifts with those who need them most.

The irony in living your life this way is that as you give more of your valuable assets away, you will continue to accrue more in return. The amount of time Phil has given to children and what he feels he has received in return is a perfect example. The more he receives, the more he must give away. This is the very reason why so many people have benefited from Phil's time and gifts.

When I stated at the beginning of the chapter that living life successfully was a lifestyle rather than a destination, I was thinking of people like Phil Smart. Phil is not successful because he has lots of money, recognition, respect, and admiration. He is not successful because of what he has *received* from the world. Phil is successful because of what he has *given* back to the world. With Phil, it truly is not the duration but the donation that makes him unique. The measurement of his life is that he will be sorely missed when he is gone.

Recently, Phil was asked to make a presentation to the student body at Aberdeen High School in Washington. When he was finished and the gymnasium was empty, a young female student approached him with tears in her eyes and said, "Mr. Smart, I want to be just like you." Humbled and flattered, he responded by telling her the truth. He explained that she had been born just like him with unique gifts and talents all her own. All she had to do was choose to use her gifts in a way that gave back to others. It is my hope that, like that young lady, we will all aspire to be truly successful in the way Phil has modeled.

All of us may not have the capacity to give material objects to others, but everyone has the same amount of time. The greatest sacrifice you can make is to give of your own precious, personal time. How are you spending your third eight?

Are you willing to share the gifts that have been given to you? Any one of us, regardless of our circumstances, can find some way to give back. Make a phone call to someone who needs encouragement. Volunteer at the homeless shelter. Do something kind for your neighbor without expecting anything in return. Donate money or merchandise to the needy. It doesn't take much to change a life. And when you share your gifts with those that need them most, you will receive the fulfillment that comes from positively changing the world. That is everlasting success.

13

MY DREAMS FOR THE FUTURE

"Life is as successful as you choose to live it."

It is my vocational dream to support my family doing what I feel passionate about. That is, to travel the country—eventually with my wife, once the kids are grown—communicating to youth and adults that the future is what you make it. I am very concerned with the depression and anxiety that many people struggle with in life, and my heart aches for those most vulnerable—our teenagers. The feeling of hopelessness for the future, which permeates this generation, is leading kids to make all sorts of unhealthy choices without consideration for their future or anyone else's. Life has become meaningless for those trapped without any hopes or dreams for tomorrow.

It is my desire to motivate people to understand that life is as successful as you choose to live it, regardless of your current situation, and that there are proven steps you can take to make yours successful, if you are willing to try. I have been blessed with many different experiences in my young life, including my amputation, which have taught me a great deal. I have also had opportunities to learn invaluable lessons from wise people I have known, and am continuing to learn more everyday. And now I believe I have been given the gift of effectively communicating ideas—of motivating those who hear me to take action. It is my plan to share what I have learned with as many people as possible, either by speaking to them personally or through my writings and other media.

I believe strongly that I can and will achieve my dream. Thus far, I have been successful in encouraging thousands of people through school assemblies, and community and business presentations. This book is just one of the many I hope to write.

Beyond my vocational aspirations, my dream is to watch my children grow and experience joyful, fulfilling, successful lives. Pam and I are attempting to teach them to make the most of every opportunity and to consider the consequences of every decision on the way to their dreams. We want them to know that they are never too old to be dreamers and doers, and the accomplishment of one dream just leads to the thrill of looking forward to the next. We try to teach by example that success in life is not what you get, but what you give.

As for Pam and me, we dream of living the rest of our lives together, growing in love and respect for one another every single day. We believe it is worth the pain of working hard to continue to overcome any differences of opinion or shortcomings in our relationship.

I have left my most heartfelt dream for last because it is the most important. My greatest dream is that every person I come in contact with will be able to confidently answer the following question for themselves: *Why am I even here*?

14

WHY AM I HERE?

"There must be more to this life than what we can see."

It may have been appropriate for this final chapter to have been the first. I believe that until we can answer one fundamental question of our existence, we will never find true meaning and purpose for the time we spend on planet earth. The question which we must all answer for ourselves and in our own way is *Why am I even here*? If we are unable to find the right answer to this question, everything we have discussed in this book becomes meaningless.

All that we have considered in these pages—the principles, actions, and attitudes—are helpful to living a successful life during the time we are here. But, is this the end? The philosopher in me leads me to occasionally look at life from an analytical viewpoint. I like to dig below the surface of a situation and try to find the meaning behind it. When considering the 70-plus years I hope to live on this earth, I am constantly brought back to the conclusion that there must be more to this life than what we can see.

Scholars are continually finding new evidence and developing new theories that disprove previous scientific theories concerning the beginning of time and our existence. When it comes to the question of how did the earth, and ultimately mankind, begin, I am amused at how many times the great thinkers of the world continue to disprove the great thinkers that preceded them. The great minds of this generation will surely be proved wrong by the next when it comes to theories of the beginning of time. I believe it takes great faith to believe that the entire universe and its inhabitants were created by some sort of interstellar accident. If the earth was formed as a result of some rock floating through space, where did the rock come from? It is much easier for me to acknowledge the existence of a creator with a purpose.

So, why are we here? The answer must be searched for and finally uncovered by you. I cannot answer the question for you, I can only share what I believe to be true. The answer to this question for my life is the foundation on which I build my hopes and dreams for the future. It is the only thing that can bring me lasting peace, joy, encouragement, and purpose. And I joyfully share it with you for your consideration.

I have had enough experiences that have been spiritual in nature to convince me that we are spiritual beings. The rest I take on faith in God's Word, the Holy Bible, and the undeniable historical evidence which supports its teachings.

I believe with my whole heart that I am here because of a God who created me and the world I live in. I further believe that I was created to have a relationship of mutual love with him and that he has given me the ability to choose my own dreams, goals, and decisions for this life. I have even been given the choice of whether or not I will love him.

It is my belief that he loves me so much, that even when I reject his love or his existence, he's willing to forgive me and still wants me to live with him forever. When my time on this earth is over, he will take me to a home he has prepared for me.

The greatest news is that he is preparing a place for every one of us, and it is free. We can do nothing to earn this everlasting life. He has already purchased our ticket to get in. We don't have to join the "Christian Club" or do good works and never sin. It is a free gift that is ours for the asking.

We must simply acknowledge and accept that our Creator loved us so much that even when we rejected him by our sin, an act that carried the penalty of separation from God forever, he forgave us. He sent his own son, Jesus Christ, to this earth to live a perfect life, then suffer and die in our place as payment of the penalty for us. But after dying for our sins, Christ rose from the dead and went to be with our Heavenly Father, just as we will by our faith in him. He did all of this so that by believing it to be true and accepting it as a personal fact for our lives, after death our new bodies and our spirits will be brought together to live forever with God in heaven.

God has instructed us through Jesus Christ that our purpose here is twofold. First, we are to love God with all our heart, soul, and mind. Second, we are to love our neighbor as much as we love ourselves. Because of his great love and sacrifice for me, I strive to choose dreams, goals, and decisions that honor him and nurture healthy relationships with others. Not because I have to, but because I want to. He is the creator of the universe and he has called me to be an heir to his kingdom. All the wealth on this earth cannot begin to compare with the inheritance my Father God has for me.

The inheritance is there for the asking. And you are invited to accept it. If you want to claim the inheritance of your Creator, say this simple prayer:

Heavenly Father, I have been searching for hope and meaning for my life. I have felt pain and sorrow at times and need to be comforted. I acknowledge that you are the creator of the universe and you have a plan for me. I believe that your son, Jesus Christ, suffered and died to purchase my forgiveness. God, I ask you for that forgiveness for all of the things I have ever done to dishonor you. Jesus, I invite you to fill my heart and live in me. Give me the peace that you have promised. Thank you for accepting me into your Heavenly Family. Give me the strength to live in a manner that honors you. Bless my hopes and dreams. I look forward to seeing you face to face, God, and thanking you for the gift of your only son. Amen.

If you prayed that prayer and meant it, you have an inheritance that will never pass away. You are a joint heir to the throne of God. When you know there is such a happy ending, it is certainly much easier to get excited about life and the future available to us. Now go out and behave in a manner worthy of your calling.

ABOUT TRUE COLORS

Our vision at True Colors is to foster positive and productive schools and communities whose successes flow from the natural dedication of each person. Our powerful, customized "edutainment" workshops, training sessions, books, workbooks, videos, live shows and events have empowered millions of people during the past twenty years and helped to realize this vision.

True Colors "edutainment" always begins with an easy, fun "who-am-I?" color card game that keys people to the four basic character traits that make each of us unique. Through innovative, interactive activities, participants learn to communicate their newly described selves in virtually any personal and professional situation. Our positive, revolutionary approach results in dramatically improved and successful lives.

To order additional copies of this book or to request more information about True Colors services & products:

True Colors, Inc.
12395 Doherty Street, Riverside, California 92503
Telephone: (800) 422-4686 or (909) 371-3901
Facsimile (909) 371-1701
E-Mail: info@truecolors.org
Web Site: www.truecolors.org